A *Life* REMEMBERED

DEBORAH ANN O'NEIL

NEWMAN SPRINGS PUBLISHING
320 Broad Street
Red Bank, NJ 07701

First originally published by Newman Springs Publishing 2020

ISBN 978-1-64801-299-0 (Paperback)
ISBN 978-1-64801-300-3 (Digital)

Printed in the United States of America

For as long as I can remember in my adulthood, I have been pushed, guided, and encouraged to write. From my parents, grandmother, children, husband, and close friends, I decided to take that chance and listen. It is to you that I dedicate this book!

Contents

Preface

When I first considered writing this book, I struggled with the names for the characters (fictional or real) as well as how deeply I should go into my story, and the list went on and on. For years, I jotted down ideas and toyed with being open and honest about my life's ups and downs, and then I finally came to the realization that if I can help just one person in their struggles get through the pain by being honest, then that was the best way to approach this story.

And so I began the journey of unveiling my trials and tribulations as well as my joyous moments to you, the reader. My hope is that you will experience those moments and take away from each chapter something that may help you as you go through your own life experiences. I hope as you read this book, you laugh and even cry, but in the end, you come to realize there is an inborn strength within each one of us, so dig deep, find it, and never be knocked down again! *Never!*

My main purpose for this book is to help others realize their own uniqueness and talents that you bring into the world. Don't ever allow anyone to cause you to doubt your worth. Never give up and always remember that change begins with *you.*

Chapter 1

THE WOMEN WHO
MADE ME WHO I AM

Our most treasured heirlooms are
the memories of our family.

The birth of a baby—how exciting, how captivating. As the proud parents and relatives gather around the nursery, peering in the nursery window and making their comments as to whom she most resembles in the family, this little one has taken center stage. Her entrance has impacted so many lives, more than she could ever imagine. Whom she looks like is really of no importance. She is her own person, filled with unlimited opportunities to make her unique mark on the world.

And so my life begins to unfold. As I entered this world in Pennsylvania in the late 1940's to middle-class parents, my soul mate was making his entrance approximately 262 miles away in Amsterdam, New York, to an equally excited family.

First child, first grandchild, first great grandchild in a strong line of women on my mother's side would turn out to be one of the greatest gifts I inherited. My great grandmother, whose birth name was Eveline Prudence Page, a name that sounds like a wealthy aristocrat that came right out of a novel, was far from wealthy in the material sense. She had been a Governess in England, but after her husband passed away, she knew she needed to find a better way to support her children, and so her journey to America began. Leaving behind all that was familiar to her, a single mother at the age of twenty-nine, took her four children, three girls—Mary, Katherine, Eveline, ages five, four, and three—along with one boy, John, age ten months, and departed together on a long journey across the ocean on the S. S. *Merion* on March 26, 1908 for a new land and a new life, hopefully a better one than the one she just left. They arrived tired and hopeful into the Port of Philadelphia on April 10, 1908.

Times were tough here in America for her, and at one point, it was even suggested that she place her four small children into an orphanage, to which she vehemently refused. She was more determined now to be an even better mother and provider for her children as no one was going to take these children away from her. They survived the long trip across the ocean, and they would survive now. She took on various jobs, hand sewing for people as well as working in a knitting factory for many long hours. In the end, her efforts were rewarded, and her family remained together. Eventually, she remarried, lifting some of the burdens from her shoulders.

Growing up with this remarkable lady helped form who I am today. She never complained about her hardships or showed bitterness for the many struggles she faced.

Her lessons were taught not only in her words but through her actions her entire life. She stressed the importance of family and working hard to get what you want because it is only then that you truly come to appreciate what you have. Nothing is more gratifying than working and saving to acquire what you need or desire. There is a different appreciation for things that you worked for rather than what was simply given to you. These lessons are deeply rooted into my way of living and thinking.

My grandmother Mary, who was the oldest daughter, reflected so much of her mother's teachings. She followed in her footsteps working in factories and saving for the things that she wanted. She learned the skills from her mother such as knitting, crocheting, and sewing, a skill that unfortunately escaped both my mother and me.

I referred to my grandmother as Nanny. She had three children: two boys, Edward and Joseph, and a daughter, Evelyn. Her daughter was my mother.

Nanny had her share of heartaches during her lifetime. She suffered the loss of her firstborn son shortly after he was born in the hospital, survived the Great Depression, survived TB, and was the caretaker of my grandfather for many years after suffering from a massive stroke.

Putting my grandfather into a nursing home was not an option for her. I was a teenager when he had his stroke, and I chose to give up my bedroom so that he could have his privacy, never thinking twice about this decision. The décor quickly changed from a girly teenager's room—accented with hues of purple on the walls and bedspread, carpeting on the floor, and photos that adorned the bureau of family and friends—to a simple room with soft blue walls, a hospital bed, and hospital equipment placed on hardwood floors.

Prior to his stroke, he had been a workaholic. My Pop Pop instilled in my brother and me values, a strong work ethic, and a firm belief that hard work was something you did if you wanted to be successful. We were reminded by him that nothing was free in this world. He was a roofer, and he did not know how to relax. Even while on vacation at the New Jersey shores, he would find some side jobs to do.

His stroke was debilitating. He was left paralyzed on one side and lost his ability to speak. How frustrating it must have been for him to be reduced to this, especially being a man who once was so active. His mind was as sharp as a tack; it was his body that now failed him. He was locked inside this body, unable to move or speak. The torment of having all your facilities and not being able to follow through with what your mind is telling you had to be heartbreaking. All that he had now was his family, who dearly loved him.

My Nanny was a ray of sunshine, always had a smile on her face and a kind word for everyone. She became known as the party girl, the bell of the ball. She never sat still when music started playing. All ages danced with her, and she loved the attention. She had a particular flair on the dance floor that people sat in awe, watching her as she gracefully moved about the floor. She knew how to enjoy life. The party didn't begin until she arrived. She never needed a drink to loosen her up before dancing, although she enjoyed one. She felt the music, her feet were always tapping, and she was eager to get out there on the dance floor. I, unfortunately, did not inherit this from her as I was shy and self-conscious when it came to getting up and dancing. I am more on the reserved side, more like my great-grandmother and mother.

Growing up, my brother and I benefitted from Nanny's free spirit. Our mother was extremely protective, too cautious many times, so when Nanny watched us, she taught us how to be more daring and to explore our surroundings. She taught us how to safely cross the street, making sure to look both ways before we went to play with our friends. When we fell off our bikes, she'd get us right back up and watch us ride as if nothing ever happened. This woman gave us the courage to stand up for ourselves, laugh at ourselves, and explore our surroundings without fear. She had a unique way of comforting us when we were upset or worried about something. Her style wasn't one for giving lots of hugs and kisses, nor was she like most other grandmothers who always were pinching your cheeks every chance she got. We knew she loved us in spite of her feeling awkward in displaying too much affection. Her ways to express her love were shown through her baking, reading us stories, knitting sweaters, mending clothes, playing with us, helping with homework, and always being there whenever we needed her.

She was an excellent baker, making everything from scratch. The house always smelled so good when we came home from school from freshly baked chocolate chip cookies to my favorite homemade lemon meringue pie. With the leftover dough, she would make us our very own mini pastry filled with our favorite flavored jam/jelly. This was Nanny's way of saying, "I love you," and these memories still live on today.

She was a funny lady who loved Halloween. She would dress up every year, many times better than my brother or me. Proudly, she would go knocking on neighbors' doors in full costume with her trick or treat bag in hand. Every neighbor looked forward to her entrance. Where there was laughter, there was Nanny.

Nanny always wanted to return to England, her birthplace, to visit the home where she was born and walk the streets once again where she so innocently played as a child. My parents granted her this wish, which she talked about for many years. We take for granted living in the country where we were born, being able to visit the hospital where we were born, the house that we lived in as a young child, or the schools that we attended. So I can only imagine how exciting it was for her to be able to go back to her earlier days and reminisce on that time in her life.

She battled illnesses throughout her life, and yet she never let her family see the pain or fear that she endured. In her younger years, she suffered from TB when I was just born and had a portion of her lung removed. She later had to deal with breast cancer, going through radiation and chemo. The radiation treatments were so bad that her chest was badly burned, leaving that area looking and feeling like a piece of leather. It is terrible to watch loved ones suffer like this, but she was determined that she would not give in to cancer, and so she fought. She won that battle for many years, but in the end, cancer returned, and I lost a very dear and loving person in my life.

As she was dying in her hospital bed, surrounded by her loved ones, she told me that she wanted me to have her necklace, the one that I had given her when I had my first job. The necklace was shaped like a sunburst with a small diamond in the center. Nanny wore that necklace from the first day that I gave it to her, never taking it off; and now, she was passing it onto me.

There was a strange feeling that came over me, one that scared me because I sensed at that moment that this would be the last time that I would spend with my Nanny. I pressed my face next to hers, kissed her repeatedly, and told her how much she was loved. She whispered to me that she loved me too, and then she drew her last breath. She waited for me to be there by her bedside, to say our goodbyes and to tell me that she loved me. I loved her dearly and was richly blessed having her for my very own grandmother. The void in my heart is always there, but so are the lessons that she taught me.

Being Nanny, she told us all that when she comes back, she is coming back as a bird and crapping (she really said shitting) on everyone's car who ever annoyed her for whatever reason. Some days, when there were bird droppings on my car, I'd look up at the heavens and ask her, "What did I do, Nanny?" and chuckle.

And then there was my mother, Evelyn, who was so sweet, caring, and so dedicated to her family. She had two children, Debbie (me) and Eddie. She was the matriarch of our family, making sure that her family sat at the dinner table each night, shared the events of the day, watched TV together, played board games after dinner or on rainy days (Monopoly, Clue, Life, Twister, Scrabble, Checkers, to name a few), and was very much involved in my brother's and my life. She, along with my father taught us respect, responsibility, and loyalty to family.

It was easier to get away with things from my father than my mother. She rarely accepted excuses for things not getting done and took a no-excuse approach when it came to homework. We knew when we came home from school that we needed to get our written homework done before dinner, or don't even waste our time asking to go outside with our friends later in the evening. Our parents checked our homework after we completed it and signed it.

My brother and I had one job and that was being good students, and our parents made sure that was happening. They quizzed us before we had a test and spent time going over what it was that we didn't understand. If we were absent from school because we were sick or played being sick, that meant we couldn't go out after school or even be on the phone if by chance we had a miraculous recovery during the course of the day. We both soon learned that it was far better to go to school than stay at home.

On the other hand, every morning, before getting ready for school, Mom woke us up with a hot cup of tea and a piece of buttered toast to start our day at our bedside. Who needed or even wanted an alarm clock when you could be woken up every morning with such love?

Mom was a career woman—smart, dedicated, a professional—working as an executive Secretary, helping my father pay the bills and providing us with the nicer things in life, but she never once lost sight of what was really important, and that was her family. Together, they worked and saved to purchase a new home, one that was built to their specifications. It was exciting as a child to visit the site of our new home, watching it go up a little at a time, and then finally moving into it. We had lived in the city, which was busy and noisy with traffic, and now we were moving into a section of the city that was less travelled and quiet.

The new neighborhood was a perfect place to grow up in. Neighbors were caring and friendly and watched out for each other's children. There was a kinship with the neighbors. Everyone looked after each other, never invading the others privacy; rather, acting with genuine concern for the members in the community. This is something that is lost today. In this busy world where everyone has so much on their mind and so much to do, neighbors have become nothing more than people you greet in passing. Some of my fondest memories are from those early years, when a friendly neighbor's face greeted me when I got off the school bus with a warm dish of home-made chocolate chip cookies and a cold glass of milk. Her willingness to listen to how my day went at school, while filling my glass of milk and adding a few more cookies to my plate, made being a kid extra special.

Family and friends meant everything to my mother. She was always thinking about others, never forgetting anyone's birthday or anniversary. She had a card for every occasion and never let an event go unnoticed. I inherited that gift from her. I often thought that I should own a Hallmark card store with all the cards that I send. Family gatherings with all the special table arrangements and decorations, coupled with their favorite foods, were a part of every holiday. China and crystal graced her holiday table as paper products were never permitted unless it was a picnic that she was hosting. My mother entertained effortlessly, or so it appeared, but those who lived with her knew the hours of preparation and planning that went into every event. She was an elegant woman and a gracious hostess. When you were invited to Evelyn's home, you felt welcome and part of her family.

My brother and I were taught responsibility. We had chores—I set the table each night, my brother took out the trash, and my parents did the dishes. That was their quiet time to talk about their day while my brother and I went out to play until the streetlights went on. As I got older, I then would put the dinner in the oven, peel the potatoes, and prepare whatever vegetables we were having that night so when our parents pulled up from work, all they needed to do was mash the potatoes and serve dinner. Each one played their part in our family dynamics to help one another and enjoy our time together gathered at the dinner table.

Music echoed throughout the house. The stereo played a broad genre of songs, and you would undoubtedly catch our parents dancing to Frank Sinatra, Kenny Rogers, to name a few. Even to this day, I work around the house listening to music from my earlier childhood days and smile.

Respect for God, our country, our elders, and ourselves were part of our raising, and sad to say, something that I feel is lost today. We were always taught to say "please" and "thank you," to open the door for an adult, to remove ourselves when adults were speaking and never interrupt without saying "excuse me," to address an adult not by their first name but by using Miss, Mr., or Mrs., unless they told us to call them something else.

The strength from the women in my past continued to shine through with my mother. She was always afraid of getting cancer, especially since her mother and her mother's mother passed away from this deadly disease. But instead of being proactive, she chose to avoid going for yearly checkups for fear she'd be given the news that she most feared: cancer. Her fear caused her to neglect the noticeable (lump in her breast), and when she finally brought it to her doctor's attention, it was too late and too far gone. The tumor was the size of a grapefruit and required extensive surgery. Given the news that she feared all her life, she suffered a heart attack. Once recovered from the heart attack, she underwent a radical mastectomy.

During her recovery, a nurse took her blood pressure and blood from her arm (side where she had the mastectomy), causing her arm to blow up three times its normal size, never to return to normal. Not only did she have to face losing her breast, going through chemo treatments, but now she had the added burden of dealing with a sore oversized arm. At night, she required a pillow to rest her arm to sleep; and in the summer, she did not wear short sleeves as she was so embarrassed by its size, so she covered it up with long sleeve blouses. This lovely and fashionable woman endured a great deal and never once complained to her family. What she and my father discussed about her illness, her children never knew. My dad was there wholly and entirely for my mother, and he always made her feel beautiful.

At first, we thought she might have beaten this horrible disease as she was seven years cancer free, but it surfaced its ugly head and struck my mother again, this time attacking her lungs. How difficult it must have been for her to deal with this horrid disease yet again and to know that this would cause her life to be cut short. She kept on her nightstand a saying, which she lived by: "Let Go—Let God." She did not want to be in a hospital or hospice, as her mother had been. She prayed that she would die peacefully at home, with my father nearby. God answered her prayers, and my mother passed away peacefully (at age sixty-one) in her bed beside my father.

The loss of my mother is indescribable, but the comfort in knowing that she died peacefully at home with my father at her side gives me some comfort. This loss occurred two years after my Nanny's passing, and once more, I felt alone and lost. The special women in my life, who always were there for me, were now gone forever, or at least physically, but I know they are always around me to protect, encourage, and support me. I feel their presence, especially when I am at my lowest and need their love and guidance.

I recall that dreadful night when my dad called, sobbing to say that my mom had passed away. I felt like the life went out of me—I fell to the floor, phone in hand, and told my dad I'd be right there. How I was able to drive to the house, I can honestly say I don't know. God had to be the one steering the car that night, as I was in shock. I just was told the woman whom I loved and cherished was now gone—gone forever. Oh, God, how can I make it without her?

I ran into the house, my Dad still holding her, as I entered the bedroom. Our family doctor and dear friend was called to the house, and when I saw him, all we could do was cry. What words could I say to my dad right now that would give him some comfort? There

17

were none. He just lost his love, his first love and his soul mate. I felt so helpless.

This house would never be the same. The home I grew up in surrounded with love and laughter was a thing of the past. My mother was the key player in making our house a home, and now she was gone. Something that still haunts me to this day is the sound of the zipper as the bag was closing, holding my mother to be led away, and the chill that filled the air as she was wheeled down the hallway. That zipper sound replayed itself over and over for a long time. I could not wrap my mind around the fact that our time together was over. I wept as our doctor held me and covered my face so that I wouldn't see my mother leaving her home in that bag on that stretcher. He wanted me to remember my mother the way she was and not like this. To this day, I am eternally grateful for his presence of mind and for doing this. Our doctor was a good friend, and his heart was as sad as ours.

I knew what my mother liked and how she liked things done, so I gathered up my strength, and I worked on her funeral arrangements with my dad's support. I was friendly with one of my daughter's teachers at school, so together, we created her mass booklet. We searched for just the right verses to be read, the music to be played, the flowers to surround her. We wanted the song "Wind Beneath My Wings" by Bette Midler to be sung, but the church wouldn't approve it because it wasn't a hymn but suggested we use "On Eagle's Wings" as her exit from church, which we did.

The song "Wind Beneath My Wings" always reminded her of my dad and how supportive he had been during her most difficult times, which is why I really wanted that particular song. In between many tears, I was able to finish this task, and her funeral was both beautiful and eloquent, just like her. The funeral director told us afterward that she had one of the most interminable processions they ever saw, except for a dignitary. I knew she was proud of how her final journey went because at the cemetery, butterflies were flying all around, which my dad and I quickly noticed. To understand how we knew she was pleased, my mother always said that "she would come back as a butterfly, graceful and free."

Every time my dad or I would see a butterfly, we knew it was her. She was stopping by to visit and let us know that she is still with us. She loved butterflies, so whenever I see them—large or small, plain white/yellow or quite colorful—fluttering in my garden, I stop and say, "Hi, Mom. I love and miss you still." I look forward to my butterfly greetings as I work in my garden or visit her at the cemetery. On one occasion when I was placing flowers on her grave, a monarch butterfly flew over my head, circled back, and then brushed my face. I fell to my knees and cried like a baby, sitting there for over an hour, lost in my thoughts of yesteryear. I found a sense of peacefulness there, free to grieve and reflect on our lives together.

I visit my mother's grave site often and place a new floral arrangement there, along with an American flag, when I go. She would tell me whenever we visited my grandparents' grave site to place flowers for the holidays and noticing plastic flowers on other sites, "When I pass away, don't ever put plastic on my grave. I'd rather nothing than plastic, and if you do, I'll reach right up out of the ground and toss them away." We would laugh at her whenever she said this because she rarely joked. But let me tell you this: we have never put plastic flowers on her grave site—*never*. Even my children, her grandchildren, know that story, and they only use real flowers or silk floral arrangements for the holidays.

I recall one Christmas when my dad and I were buying the blanket and wreath for her grave site, and all they had on the blanket were plastic poinsettias. We looked at each other, laughed, and bought the blanket. We came home, cut off the plastic flowers, and replaced them with vibrant red silk poinsettias. Then we headed to the cemetery. So you can see, that's how much we believed what she told us years ago. She was still in charge, even in death.

I've come to learn that you need to treasure each and every precious moment that you share with your loved ones. Take nothing for granted because you never know what tomorrow will bring. It's a lesson that I can hopefully pass on to you, the reader. There is nothing more special, more cherished, than time spent with family and friends. These are the memories that help you through when that special person is no longer with you, for without these, your life is empty and cold. I've been blessed, and my memories of those I cherish are many. This is how I get through some of the darkest times.

The void in my life, the pain that gnaws at my heart, is still very new. So often, I want to pick up the phone or stop by the house to ask her opinion about something or get a much-needed hug, and then the horrible realization steps in, and I know those moments are forever gone. No one can truly understand how painful it is to bury a parent unless you have lost one yourself. No matter how old you are, you always want to know that you can turn to your mother and have a question answered or get comfort when you are in pain.

How many times do you want your mother to be there with you when you are sick or feel sad? Something about the power of a good mother! I miss my mother terribly, but somehow, I think she is still with me. When I am at my lowest, I stop and talk to her, sometimes asking for a sign that she hears me, and find comfort.

If you are lucky enough to still have your mother, make sure you take the time to tell her that she is loved, and enjoy the simple things, like just being in her company, for sadly, the day will inevitably come when she won't be there anymore, and you too will feel the void that I have without my mother.

Chapter 2

MY FATHER

My father didn't tell me how to live; he
lived and let me watch him do it.
—Clarence B. Kelland

I couldn't continue with my story without talking about my dad. There aren't enough adjectives to accurately describe this man. He was a dedicated son, grandson, brother, husband, father, grandfather, and friend. During his childhood, he faced many hardships. He didn't grow up in an affluent household, and so everyone had to pull their own weight. He was the eldest of three children, which meant that most of the burden rested on his shoulders. He had a younger brother and sister, and according to my dad, his sister was spoiled all because she was the only girl.

I'd listen to stories from his childhood, sometimes in disbelief! They didn't have a bathroom inside the house, which required them to use an outhouse. When it was bath time, he had to fill the tub with heated water so that his sister, who was supposed to be the cleanest of the three, could bathe first; and luckily, my dad was able to follow her because he was the cleaner of the two boys. His younger brother was last to bathe as he was by far the dirtiest. When everyone finished their bath, it was his job to empty the bath water and clean up.

Those old stories that you'd hear about putting paper inside your shoes because there was a hole in your shoe, I came to learn was a fact. Until his parents could afford a new pair for him, he learned how to make do. There was no complaining or arguing.

Speaking of shoes, my dad told me another story about the time my mother bought him a new pair of shoes, but they were half a size too small. He never said a word to her that they weren't the correct size but instead would squeeze his foot into the shoe. He confessed that he only wore them occasionally as they hurt, and to avoid hurting my mother, he chose to hide the shoes in the deepest corner of his closet with other shoes neatly placed in front of them. I learned this secret when I was cleaning out the closet after my mother's passing and donating things that were hers as well as clothes that my father no longer needed or wanted since retiring. When I came across the box with these infamous shoes inside, I asked him why he had them stuffed in the back of the closet since they looked like they were never worn, and that is when the truth came out. Hopefully, someone is enjoying these stylish shoes today.

Education was of the utmost importance to him. He never missed a day of school from first grade up through high school until his grandfather passed away, and he took that day off to honor him and attend his funeral. These values are what defined him. He took nothing for granted and appreciated everything, no matter how small. So I can only imagine the excitement and joy that filled his heart when he was able to give his children a new home.

The first home was a row home in Philadelphia, which cost five thousand dollars. It required my dad to work two jobs to purchase. The neighborhood was predominately white yet diverse in nationality and religion. It was this home where I was born; and three years later, my brother joined me.

The second home was even more exciting and rewarding for my dad as this one was being built brand-new with all the specifications my parents requested. Located in Northeast Philadelphia, the purchase of this home required two incomes, both my father's and my mother's. It was beautiful, and it was here that my brother and I spent our childhood.

I would often sit by my dad and ask him questions about his life, his hopes and dreams, and his views on life. What I took away from these conversations gave me a deeper understanding of the man I so lovingly called Dad.

Tech Sgt. Edward A. Vollmer Sr. back row, second from the right.

My dad—a thin young nineteen-year-old, 5'8.5" tall and weighing all of about 130 pounds—enlisted in the United States Air Force on November 7, 1942, ready to serve his country. He arrived in England, May of 1943, assigned to the 8th Air Force. He was part of the 100th Bomb Group, known as the Bloody Hundredth, the most famous massive bomb group of World War II. His role was a tail gunner TG (T), flying over twenty missions over Germany in a B-17, known as the Flying Fortress. His B-17 Flying Fortress became an icon and symbol of the Air Force during World War II. He served many tours during the war and yet spoke very little about these historical times where he was a key player.

I learned through my school years that this war was considered to be the deadliest conflict in human history and that the B-17 had dropped more bombs than any other US aircraft in that war. There has never been a war like World War II, and this was my dad's service years. He was witness to much destruction and heartache, and although he was the recipient of the Silver Star, Purple Heart, EAME with two Battle Stars, Distinguished Flying Cross, Air Medal with five Oak Leaf Clusters. He never considered himself to be a hero.

He was struck with shrapnel during one mission on January 10, 1944, and it was his dog tags that saved his life. He claims no fame for this mission; instead, he said he was doing his duty, as any American would do to protect his homeland. When I asked about his many medals, he merely stated that many others were more deserving than he. With all of these accomplishments, my dad has always said that his most significant achievement was being a father.

Honorably Discharged on September 23, 1945 as a Technical Sergeant from Lowry Field, Colorado, his new life as a civilian would begin. The war was finally over, but those memories of his time far away from his homeland will forever be etched in his mind.

Unlike the early childhood memories that he so freely shared with me, his military memories seemed to be his and his alone. These memories were locked away in his mind, and there they would stay. I didn't learn of his heroic tales from my dad. It was through textbooks, movies, and notes I found in his service journal that he kept on his missions where I indeed learned of the dangers he faced and the patriotism that he so proudly felt.

Humility was a trait that he genuinely possessed. His was a unique generation, one of service, loyalty, and humility. Even when we took a trip to Washington, DC, to tour the War Memorial, he said very little. His eyes teared up when he stood by the wall that paid tribute to the European Company he so proudly served, which read,

THE WAR'S END—TODAY THE GUNS ARE SILENT. A GREAT TRAGEDY HAS ENDED. A GREAT VICTORY HAS BEEN WON. THE SKIES NO LONGER RAIN DEATH—THE SEAS BEAR ONLY COMMERCE—MEN EVERYWHERE WALK UPRIGHT IN THE SUNLIGHT—THE ENTIRE WORLD IS QUIETLY AT PEACE.

It was a somber moment, and I knew not to ask questions, so I quietly reached for his hand, held it in mine, and told him how much I loved him. He squeezed my hand, smiled, and told me he loved me too.

Many unspoken moments occurred that day, and I knew in my heart that he was grateful that this country showed the vets how much they appreciated the sacrifices these brave men and women had given to keep us free and safe, and that was all I needed. I think back to that day, now that my dad is gone, that this trip that I planned with him was probably one of the best gifts that I could have given him. He knew how proud I was, that I was aware of the many sacrifices made, and that I respected his wishes to keep these memories to himself. And after reading his handwritten notes in his journal from those war days, I came to understand why it was such a difficult topic to discuss.

Although he never saw himself as an American Hero, everyone else did. He was honored by a friend of my daughter's, who also served in the United States Air Force, when she had a flag given to him that flew over the skies of Iraq in support of Operation Iraqi Freedom on March 23, 2006 aboard E-8C JSTARS aircraft #02-9111 in his honor. He was a very proud American. He cherished that flag and kept it safe, along with the plaque.

He flew the flag every day out front of his home and would remind my brother and me that we had to vote because that was a freedom that he, along with so many others, boldly fought for and that we must never take that freedom for granted. He stressed how blessed we were to live in the land of the free.

My Uncle Joe, my dad's brother-in-law, was fascinated about the missions my dad had flown, which drove him to engage in some additional research. He began researching each mission and soon was able to contact many of the servicemen who had flown with my dad. My dad identified the various servicemen in the photos, and my uncle took it from there. Connections soon happened, opening the doors for many correspondences and memories. Some of the men had since passed away, but those who were still alive shared their lives once again with one another. For some, it was their children who reconnected with my dad, trying to get answers to the questions they had, which never were answered. He gave those family members some closure and responded to their many letters, answering as many questions as he could. Reading his daily journal, along with the questions that he answered for the servicemen's families, brought this war to life for me in a way no one else could or ever would.

Chapter 3

CHILDHOOD

Childhood is the most beautiful of all seasons.

M y parents married the day after Christmas, when my dad was serving in the Air Force. For the remainder of his tour, he and my mother were together in Denver. My mother had never been away from home before, and this was a bit overwhelming for her, especially since she was a newlywed, but it didn't take her long to adjust and make new friends. She always had a way with people. As time went on, I came to realize that this too was something that I had in common with my mother our love of family and the need to be close to home, as well as enjoying new people that entered into my world.

When my dad's tour was over, both he and my mother returned home and began planning for a family. Month after month, they hoped for a miracle, which turned into years, and they were disappointed, believing that being parents was out of the question for them. The medical profession informed my parents that it could be as a result of all the missions that my dad had flown during the war at such high altitudes, but my parents refused to give up their hope of being parents. And then, something magical happened when they least expected it! My mother was pregnant with me!

Life was good for this little baby. They were attentive to my every need. No wet or soiled diapers were to be found on me. It was as if my parents and grandparents had built-in radar and were able to detect each and every time I needed a diaper change. My outfits were pristine, and should they become soiled from formula or food, they were immediately changed and placed in the wash. Clothing then needed to be ironed as most items were cotton, so my dresses were meticulously pressed and neatly placed in my closet.

More outfits were hanging on hangers than I could ever wear, or at least that is what one would think. I had a new dress on for breakfast, lunch, and dinner, ranging in color from pale green, soft shades of blue, sunny yellow, and of course girly pink. These outfits weren't randomly hung in the closet; they were all color coordinated and separated based on the seasons of the year. My mother was extremely neat and organized, where everything had its place. Having little to no hair, my mother made sure everyone knew that I was a girl, and if frilly dresses weren't enough proof of my gender, she had a matching bow placed in whatever little hair I had. There was no doubt that I was a girly girl after my mother was finished dressing me.

The years came and went, one year quickly blending into another. There were those notable first words coupled with first steps, where everyone was in awe and proudly announced to all who would listen how wonderful their little girl was. The firsts continued with dance lessons (age two), learning the ABCs, learning how to ride a two-wheeler, ice skating, roller skating, softball games, forming friendships, and first loves. These priceless memories were all recorded in baby books, photos, and videos as well as embedded forever in my parents' minds and hearts. Memorabilia was carefully and safely tucked away.

Dance lessons began at age two. I took ballet, which I detested and my mother loved, as well as tap, which I really liked. The dance recitals were a significant event in my family, but they didn't last long because my mother soon realized and accepted the fact that I really wasn't cut out to be a dancer.

My brother Eddie joined the family three years after my arrival, bringing the same excitement and joy as I had earlier. I was fortunate to have a brother to share my childhood dreams with, and our adventures took us to so many places, both real and imaginary.

Growing up in the 1950's was much like the TV shows that you see depicting that era. There was a real sense of family. Dinner was the time when we sat around the table and ate a home-cooked meal. We talked about our day and shared our stories. Playing board games was a ritual, especially the game Monopoly, where we often times played for days.

I was always looking after my little brother. When he started first grade, his class had their own spot on the ramp, separate from the rest of the school since they were the youngest. Eddie would place his lunch bag down on the ground inside his schoolbag and begin playing with his friends. Every day, someone would fall on his schoolbag and crush his lunch, leading him to tears. He would start calling my name from the ramp to come and fix it. My friends would alert me that my brother was crying (again), and I knew exactly why. I would head up to the ramp with my lunch in hand and swap out his crushed lunch for my perfect one. As this was becoming a daily occurrence, I decided the time had come to discuss with my parents my concerns and convince them to invest in a sturdy lunch box, one that was indestructible for my brother. What a relief when the new lunch box replaced the paper bag. I was now free to enjoy my crushed-free sandwich and cupcake.

Elementary school was typical until seventh grade. My father worked for a company that made aerial relief maps and was part of a team that was being sent overseas to another continent, which was Africa. I had only heard of these places from geography books or National Geographic, but to be told that my dad was going to live in Egypt for a year or more was foreign to me. My brother and

I were filled with many questions as we sat at the dinner table. Why did he have to leave? How long would he be gone? The whole thing seemed unreal to me as the farthest he was ever away from us was a few hundred miles. I couldn't wrap my mind around why he had accepted this offer.

Dad prepared for his departure with my mother's help, packing all the necessities, along with an address book, stamps, envelopes, and some photos. He promised that he would write to us daily, and we were going to make sure that he did by giving him all the necessary tools to do so. We took him to the airport in New York with heavy hearts, tears flowing as we said our goodbyes. We were able to walk him to his terminal and then sit by the window to watch the planes come and go. As we watched the jet take off into the clouds, I felt sick in my stomach. There was such a huge void inside. I couldn't imagine going back home without my dad.

Before long, the plane was out of sight, and the journey back home began. The ride home was quiet, except for the sobs that you could hear, even though we were trying to hide them from each other. No one uttered a word. Music on the radio didn't shed any comfort, nor did my mother's words trying to console us. I really just wanted to be alone because nothing that anyone said to me was going to make me feel better, and I knew it. My thoughts of my dad were all that I had on my mind right now.

As we entered the house late that evening, it seemed so empty. I could tell this was going to be a long six months. I went to my room and began writing to my dad. There really wasn't much in the way of news to report since I just left him, but I could tell him how much I loved him and couldn't wait for his return. And so my months of letter writing began.

We soon learned that our dad was as homesick as we were. We were a family, and that meant being together, all four of us. So when our dad called to ask if we would like to join him in Egypt, we couldn't believe it. He had rented a house in Cairo's suburbs, known as Heliopolis. He had researched and gathered all the details for our schooling should we decide to join him.

We wanted to be with our dad, but my brother and I had some reservations now that the opportunity presented itself. My brother and I liked our school, had established some close friendships both at school and in the neighborhood, and we were very close to our grandparents. On the other hand, we deeply loved our dad and didn't want to be alone without him for another year. He had already been gone for six months when he asked us to join him. He knew that this was not easy for Eddie and me and told us it was our decision and that he would understand whatever it was that we decided. Our mother was ready to jump on the next plane to join him. It was really up to my brother and me whether to stay or go.

After much thought, we knew that being a family was more important than being with friends, and so our long journey began. Preparing to go overseas was more than anyone expected. The list of things to do was daunting; passports, immunizations (there were many), gathering our records from our home school to take, reading up on a culture that was so much different than ours, shopping, booking our flights, packing our luggage, and saying goodbye to family and friends kept us busy.

Some days after school, when we headed to the doctor for our next series of shots, I recall leaving with such sore arms that I couldn't even raise them; they hurt that bad. One night in particular, when we went back to my grandparents for dinner, I was so dizzy and so sore that I could barely walk. I bumped into a large picture that was hanging in the hallway and fell to the floor. I didn't have the strength to push myself up. During the final round of immunizations, I felt so exhausted and sore that I knew I couldn't take one more needle. To be told that this was the last one was music to my ears. My mother always reminded me that these immunizations were to protect me and keep me safe from contracting any diseases overseas, but at the time, all I could think about was the pain that I was feeling.

My mother and I had to shop for clothing that was acceptable abroad. Women and girls did not wear slacks or shorts, so I had to get many sun dresses, skirts, and blouses. My wardrobe at home consisted mainly of shorts and slacks, so this was going to be a real adjustment. My brother, on the other hand, was fine with his attire.

Learning about other cultures in school was one thing, but I now had to apply what I learned and live it. This all-American girl's life was about to change.

We departed from Kennedy Airport in New York on a Trans World Airlines (TWA) 747 jet. The jet was massive, lined with so many passenger seats, none empty. There wasn't a single seat open. As we proceeded to our assigned seats, my brother and I fought for the window seat. Our mother, being the diplomat that she was, had us agree to take turns. I started out on the flight at the window, and he followed later. The window seat had its advantages, or at least I thought it did.

As the trip continued, I wasn't so sure that the window seat was the best place. Looking out the window as we began our incline up into the clouds, the people were getting smaller and smaller, as was the airport building. They were like specks on the ground, and then there was no more. Inside the plane, signs were flashing, telling all passengers to fasten their seatbelts, and the stewardesses were busy helping everyone get settled for the long flight ahead.

My ears started popping and my heart was pounding. The feeling was much different than being on a roller coaster as it ascends to the top or on an elevator as it heads to the top floor. I was being pushed so far back in my seat that my stomach felt queasy, and the flashing signs stating "Seatbelts on" made me wonder just how far up we were we going. Flying through the clouds and looking down, seeing nothing at all but blue sky, gave me such a helpless feeling that I quickly changed seats with my brother.

I could see that this was going to be a long flight, over twenty plus hours in the air. There wasn't much to keep yourself busy or occupy your time, which is why switching seats sounded like a good idea. Flying through the clouds, seeing nothing below now was somewhat eerie yet magical. How high did the sky go? I had many questions for my mother about our flight, beginning with how long it would take us to get to our destination, why did we need to change planes—and the questions just continued on and on. She patiently answered as many questions as she could, while another passenger answered the rest.

To be honest, I wasn't happy to know that we'd be in the air for over twenty hours. It wasn't like flying today with all the comforts of home with movies to watch to help pass the time. It was a very long flight, often quite bumpy, and I couldn't wait to get my feet on the ground.

As my brother and I switched seats for what seemed to be the hundredth time, placing me now back in the window seat, I noticed something black on the wing. It reminded me of the oil that my dad used in the car, so I frantically asked my mother, "What was the black stuff out there on the wing?" She leaned over to check it out, and I could sense that something wasn't right by the expression on her face. She tried brushing it off as nothing, but she quickly got up from her seat, acting like she needed to use the restroom. I saw her talking to the flight attendant, where I am sure she expressed her concern and then returned to her seat without using the restroom. It must have been something that was minor, or at least something that didn't cause much interest to the pilot because nothing was ever said or done about it.

The crew may have brushed it off, but I certainly couldn't. Every bump or dip that I felt as we flew over the ocean made me jittery, and my mind and imagination went off into some terrifying thoughts. Crashing into the ocean was uppermost in my mind, and I couldn't shake the fear that soon took over me. As for my brother, he thought each bump and dip was cool. There were no arguments now from me as to who was sitting by the window. I happily gave my brother that seat for the rest of the flight and felt relieved sitting closer to the aisle. The adults were telling us to try and get some rest, but that was impossible. Who could sleep at a time like this? Certainly not me!

The plane finally began to descend, shaking and rattling as it made its way through the clouds. The sky started to change, and instead of a vast clear blue sky with puffy white clouds, I noticed small objects below. The people and houses looked like miniature toys, making me realize just how high in the sky I was. As the plane prepared to land, so many thoughts ran through my head, and my heart was pumping so fast that I thought it would explode. The wheels touched the ground! We made it! After all the long, tedious hours in the sky, I thought how beautiful it would be to have my feet actually touch the ground. What a wonderful thought!

The doors slowly opened and it was time to make our exit. Getting up and walking around was the best feeling, even if it was only for a short time before boarding the next plane. We had to remain in the airport as our next flight was scheduled shortly after our first landing. We looked in some shops, grabbed a snack, and headed for the next plane. Looking at a map and seeing how far Egypt is from the United States doesn't compare to actually being a passenger on board taking the trip. To think about boarding another plane, ascending, and then descending was something I would rather not do, but I didn't have a choice, and so back onto the plane we went.

Thankfully, this flight wasn't as long as the first. Once seated, I was content not to have a window seat again and gave my brother that spot forever. I had enough looking out the window from a plane. Descending the plane, my legs felt like jello and I wondered how my feet were going to get me where I needed to go. Peering from the plane's door, I felt a sick feeling in the pit of my stomach as I immediately took notice of my new surroundings. The airport was smaller than the one I left from home so many hours ago, and the walls were void of any posters or advertisements. The music and sounds were unfamiliar, as was the language that the people were speaking. It was odd listening to people having a conversation and not being able to understand what they were saying. For the first time in my young life, I felt lost. As these feelings began to swell and take over my body, a familiar face appeared, and I felt comfort immediately. As my eyes met my father's, I knew at once that I was safe.

My dad had tears rolling down his face as he embraced my mother and hugged my brother and me. It was the only thing that put a smile on my face—seeing my father again. But even though my heart was happy for a brief moment, I wasn't sure this was where I wanted to be. I was scared, and I was tired. Maybe tomorrow would be better. Things are usually better in the morning. I hope this would be the case.

Chapter 4

A HOME AWAY FROM HOME

We don't miss the marble countertops and fine
linens. It's not a soft chair or bed. The reason we
miss home has nothing to do with whether it's
perfectly peaceful or happy. The reason is that
there are no strangers there, only a familiarity,
one that we take great comfort in.

A coworker of my dad's drove us back to our new home since he
was a native of the country and knew his way around as well as
the language, which was so foreign to us. Pulling up to the place that
we would be calling home for the next year or more was both odd
and intimating. It didn't feel like home. It didn't look like home. It
just simply wasn't home. With all the traveling and excitement from
the day, sheer exhaustion struck, and I finally fell asleep in my new
bedroom.

Our home, which was called a villa, reminded me more of a
castle than a house. Instead of green grass surrounding the house,
there was concrete. Instead of trees acting as a privacy wall, there was
a high concrete wall, which encased the entire house. The wall was so
high that when you walked around the property inside, you couldn't
be seen from the outside. You were closed in with an ornate wrought
iron gate that lined the entry to the house. This gate was always
locked. Scattered around the walkway were empty flower pots.

Inside the house, the furniture was larger than life and quite
ornate. Each chair was covered with different vibrant fabrics and

trimmed in gold. Nothing matched, and yet, it was quite beautiful. The prints on the chairs were different as were the designs on the sofas. It wasn't like a living room set that you would purchase in the United States, where one piece complimented the other. You would never think to mix so many colors and prints together, and yet, when you studied the room, it had a lot of character and was pleasing to the eye. The coffee tables and end tables were massive pieces of furniture. The floors were covered in beautiful ceramic tile—or maybe it was marble—with area rugs of different sizes and colors.

My first impression of this house was that it was a home for the wealthy. The walls were bare; not a single picture adorned them. They were void of any wall dressings. The living room, sitting room, and dining rooms were large enough and roomy enough to entertain a crowd. This house was definitely too big for a family of four. As I entered one room leading into the next, it became more evident that this was going to take some time getting used to before it would have that "homey feeling"—if ever.

The kitchen was large with another smaller room set off from the main kitchen. The smaller room in the kitchen area was the servant's quarters. The bedrooms were smaller in size from the other rooms in the house, except for our parent's room, which was very spacious. In some ways, I felt like Goldilocks sitting in Papa Bear's oversize chair.

In direct contrast to our home, on the corner across the street sat a straw hut, where a woman lived with her family. As time went on, we would wave to her, and she would wave back. Her straw hut was small compared to the size of our house, and her floors were nothing more than dirt. She led a simple life, and yet she and her family appeared happy. She cared for a few goats that circled her hut and grazed on the grass nearby. The goats provided her family with their milk. This frail woman operated a tiny corner store. At the store, the sign that struck me was the Coca-Cola sign, which we are all familiar with, except hers was written in Arabic. The picture on the bottle was universal—everyone knew what soda this was. Funny how things can change in appearance, but they are one in the same.

Continuing with the tour of our new home, we met a young native named Sala. He greeted us, and the interpreter informed us he was our new housekeeper (servant) and was there to assist my mother whenever she had to venture into town to go to the market. Servant? I thought my ears were playing tricks on me and so I asked my dad to clarify what this young man just said. My dad explained this it was customary here to have a servant; however, he was not to be treated as one by any of us. He was an equal and needed to be treated with respect. His purpose was to help guide us through the streets as we went to market or went shopping at the local stores. He would be helping us as we became more familiar with the customs of his country. Our dad reminded both my brother and me that we had our own chores and responsibilities here, just like we did at home. We were permitted to ask Sala questions about his country or to share our day at school with him, *but* we were never to ask him to do any chores that we were supposed to do. Dad made this very clear to us on the first day after we arrived. And so, over time, Sala became our trusted friend.

Morning came, which gave me a chance to wander outdoors and look around. Sala was right by my side, explaining what I could and could not do in the neighborhood. The villa had a massive wall surrounding it and a locked gate. From the first day, my brother and I knew that we were never to go outside the gated area without a parent or Sala. Our parents and Sala pounded this in our heads that even if we wanted to venture outside the safety of our enclosed space, we were too afraid. We heeded the warning and did not violate it. I was the one who always asked the question "why," and the answer was always the same: "It's for your safety."

Looking and listening around the neighborhood for the familiar sounds of English-speaking families was not present. I felt out of place and wondered what my school experience would be. As I was deep in thought, my dad tapped on my shoulder and told me to follow him. The family got into the car and headed for a tour of the area as well as the country club that we would call home for the next year or more.

The country club was gorgeous. The grounds, beautifully maintained, were cared for by the gardeners, cutting the thick green grass and pruning the various bushes and trees, along with the colorful flowers that surrounded the club. Sounds coming from the club were music to my ears. The people were speaking English, and the music was recognizable. I felt a huge smile come over my face, and my eyes lit up.

It continued to improve as we entered the club gates and cast our eyes on the massive Olympic-size pool, tennis courts, basketball courts, golf course, and a lovely dining area. I was introduced to several of my dad's friends from work, along with their families, who also came to join their fathers. It didn't take long before a few girls my age asked me to join them for a swim, and our friendships grew from there.

While in the confines of this club, I could be an American, able to wear shorts, flip flops, and a bathing suit. It was the closest thing to being home, and I felt comfortable there. Outside the gates of the club, there was a world that I wasn't familiar with and one that made me very uncomfortable.

The empty flower pots that surrounded our house when we first arrived soon took on a new life after my mother visited the country club. She went into town the following day with Sala and selected a wide array of beautiful colorful flowers to fill those empty pots. She watered and cared for her garden, much like the gardeners did at the club, all with her own flair and sense of style that transformed the outside of the villa immediately. She frequently made visits into town to add more color to the yard and soon earned the title of "The Flower Lady" from the vendors. Every time she passed by the vendors, they would greet her with a beautiful flower or two. She could have been our country's ambassador; she was loved by the locals that much.

It didn't take long before the signs of being homesick began to surface. One morning when I attempted to get out of bed, I was unable to lift my head from the pillow. Panic struck, and I screamed for my mother. My voice undoubtedly echoed the fear I was experiencing at that particular moment because my mother and Sala came rushing to my rescue. When my mother saw that I was paralyzed, she immediately called my father at work. Within minutes, he was at my bedside. They tried comforting me and reassuring me that I would be fine, but the expression on their faces did not match the comforting words that were coming from their mouths.

I didn't feel sick, so what was it that was making me unable to move my head? My parents were in a panic and sent for the doctor. He came to the house and ran some tests in an effort to pinpoint just what the problem was. I was scared and had a strong feeling like I would never walk again. How could I be perfectly fine one day and unable to lift my head the next? It was a mystery to everyone, including me. I was healthy back home, only to come here and be sick. What was happening?

The test results came back and indicated nothing was physically wrong, yet I still couldn't move my head. Repeated tests were taken with the same results; nothing could be found to be the cause. Finally, the doctor suggested to my parents, since all test results were negative, there was a possibility that I was homesick. He suggested that a pet may be the answer to get my mind off myself and not being home. My parents were willing to try anything. I overheard the doctor's suggestion and at first wondered how was buying me a pet going to help me lift my head again, but I wasn't going to argue because I liked the idea of getting a pet.

As the doctor continued to speak to my parents and explain his theory about my being homesick and needing something else to focus on, rather than on my sadness for being so far away from home, I nodded back off to sleep. While sleeping, they immediately went out and found me the most adorable cuddly black kitten to love. When I saw this tiny kitten, so small and in need of my love, I immediately bonded with him. I named him Sambo, and our love story began.

As parents would do, my parents began doubting whether they did the right thing by having us move to a foreign country. They were troubled by my health problems and thought about sending me back to the United States to stay with my grandparents, who were now living in our home. But just when things seemed the darkest, the sun began to shine.

Lying in bed, stroking Sambo's head, I moved my head without even knowing it. As I shifted my body to get a better grip on Sambo, who was sliding off the bed, I realized that I had just moved my head for the first time in days. I frantically yelled out to my mother and shared with her my latest development. Crying as she watched me move about in the bed, she hugged and kissed me over and over again. Not only did she shower me with hugs and kisses, but she took Sambo into her arms and began hugging and kissing him as well. Of course, Sambo, who had been accustomed to so much attention over the past few days, enjoyed every moment and purred his little heart away. He was the hero, and he had a special place in our family. My mother returned my kitten to my arms and immediately went into the living room to call my dad and relay the good news. He called the doctor to meet him at the house.

The doctor confirmed the fact that I was fine and that the problem was narrowed down to one of two things. One was the fact that I definitely was extremely homesick, and the other was the fact that I had to undergo so many immunizations in such a short period of time that this could have had something to do with being temporarily paralyzed. He told my parents that he would continually check in to keep a close watch over me for the next few months; however, it appeared the worse was over, and things should now return to normal. My dad thanked the doctor and walked him to the door.

When he returned to my room, all he could do was hug and kiss me as I wiped away the tears streaming down his face. He kept telling me how sorry he was that I had to go through this for him. He felt so responsible for my illness, and he shouldn't have. How could I let this man know that it wasn't his fault, and he wasn't to blame? What a terrible burden he carried, thinking that he was the reason I was sick. It was no one's fault, especially not my dad's. I wanted to join him in this country; he didn't force me to come. When I lifted my head from my dad's shoulder, I noticed that everyone in the room was crying, including Sala. I was a lucky girl, and I knew it. There is nothing more powerful than the power of love, and I certainly was loved.

The next morning, with the assistance of my mother, I was able to get out of bed and move slowly about the house. It was a powerful moment for me to be up and walking again. I was thrilled to be able to go from room to room in the house on my own. Of course, Sala doted on me the entire time; in fact, everyone did, including my brother.

Chapter 5

SCHOOL

School is a building which has four
walls with tomorrow inside.
—Len Watters

After a few days of getting back to normal, I was ready to begin another chapter in my life and visit my new school, Cairo American College (CAC). This school is a pre-K to 12th grade International American School located in Maadi, Cairo, Egypt. The students are mainly dependents of the local American Embassy and other international students.

There is a diverse student population. Our school was entirely different from what we were accustomed to back in the States. My brother and I were used to a school with English-speaking children, whose parents worked, like ours. Here, most of our classmates spoke several languages, whereas my brother and I spoke only one: English. These children were at a real advantage, having mastered several languages. Our instructions were in our native tongue: English; however, I was required to take a foreign language, so I chose French.

Their curriculum followed the American guidelines, such as reading, writing, math, science, social studies, music, art, and physical education; however, the requirements were more advanced. This school started teaching a second language as early as first grade, so I was behind as I only knew English. I took to learning French easier than I thought I would and was enjoying the challenge. It's a shame that we don't require and encourage learning more than one language in the United States. It really is much easier to learn at a young age rather than as a teenager or adult. It seems to come naturally to the younger ones.

Here at CAC, the teachers were serious about education and placed high expectations on each student. When I returned to the United States to begin high school, I was far more advanced than my classmates, thanks to my schooling in Egypt, and I came to realize as a freshman that I already knew the curriculum from my year in eighth grade at CAC.

My new classmates were just as nervous and scared as I was about our new school in a foreign land. We worried about making friends and being accepted by the group. Our friends were all back home, so we had to establish new friendships if we ever hoped to make it through this year. After some time, new friendships evolved, and our school experiences became less stressful. Some of these friendships continue to this very day.

Some of my fondest memories go back to Cairo American College. I learned many things not only academically, but socially as well. I was so excited to have been chosen and voted as Queen of the Valentine's Day Dance, and having the boy that I had a crush on all year to be selected as the King made it magical.

To prepare for this magical night, I needed a dress, and my mother was right on top of things. Like Cinderella's fairy godmother, she had the seamstress in town design my dress, and of course, it had to be red since this was the Valentine's Day Dance. When the evening arrived, I felt like a storybook princess. Having pictures taken at our home (aka the castle), sitting in the gold-trimmed ornate chair in our sitting room, I felt regal. This night was spectacular.

Before the dance, I was always shy and blended into the walls whenever I went to the dances. I rarely got up to dance as I was always self-conscious about being tall and thin. I was always worrying about what people thought. I had been teased about my height and weight a lot at school, but on this night, this boy, the King of the Dance, made me feel special, and I will forever be grateful to him for that. He too was tall and thin, and together we fit in.

He didn't care for dancing, and neither did I. He was a good talker and listener, and so was I. He and I managed to get through the evening because I think we were a lot alike. We realized that this evening, a friendship took off. It was a night to remember. After the dance, walking through the halls, being in class together was so much easier. I made another friend.

There were many other events throughout the year at school. Each month had some fun thing to do that brought all the kids together and allowed us to be Americans. We were able to dress like Americans without worrying about offending another's culture, and we were able to participate in games or listen to music that was uniquely American. You never realize how much you miss certain things until you have to do without them. Simple things that we as Americans enjoy back home became even more special now.

Eighth grade was a happy time, but it was coming to an end, and many of us in class were going to different schools as we were heading back to our hometowns. There was a certain sadness that I felt because these now were my friends, friends that helped pull me through a difficult time in my life when I had to adjust to a new country, new lifestyle, and make new friends. Had it not been for these special kids, my time away would have been unbearable.

Graduation was on everyone's mind, and I was no different. I wanted to graduate with my friends, whom I spent most of my elementary years with, which meant the people from home. How could this happen when I was so far from them? I knew that this was a choice that I made when I agreed to join my dad in Egypt, that I would give up my graduation in the United States, so why was I spending so much time thinking about being back home? I couldn't shake this feeling. It gnawed at me, and the more letters that came from my friends back home, the more I wished I could be there on graduation day with them.

My parents were busy preparing for my graduation, on a mission to make this day memorable. My mother, who was such a perfectionist, was searching for just the right flowers for the occasion, selecting the perfect menu that would appeal to both the adults and the graduates, and finally sending out invitations to everyone we knew. Little did I know that this party was not only my graduation celebration, but it was to be my farewell to my friends there in Egypt.

Without my knowledge, my mother had been communicating with my friends from home as well as the administrators from my former school in the United States. My mother was busy gathering the pertinent information regarding graduation—such as the time, date, and place—along with making sure that my name would appear on the program of graduates, my diploma was prepared, and that my spot would be reserved for my special day to walk with my classmates. Working hand in hand with my Nanny, my mother was busy getting all the arrangements for a graduation party in place for our return. So as the graduation celebration in this faraway land took place, I was stunned to learn that this was just the beginning of many more memorable moments in my life.

While my mother was watering her gorgeous flowers that she so carefully nurtured, my dad opened the gate to our home and asked me to sit down beside him on the step. He said that he had something important to tell me, so I was all ears. Looking into his big brown eyes, my dad took my hand and asked me a critical question. He wanted to know what I was feeling about being away from home and, more importantly, how I was feeling about missing my graduation with my friends in the United States. He told me to be honest, but I didn't want to hurt his feelings, especially since he had gone through so much with me being sick when our family first arrived, so I told him that I was okay with meeting my friends over the summer. His eyes filled up, and I thought, *Oh, God, no. He is going to tell me that we have to stay here longer.*

He repeated the question once more and directed me to tell him the truth. There was a pause before I responded this time, and I said what I was honestly feeling. I told him that I would have loved to be able to graduate with my friends back home; but if I had to choose to be with my friends or my dad, my dad would win hands down. I never expected to hear the response that my father gave, which was that I could have both...graduation from Cairo American College in Egypt as well as my graduation from Resurrection Elementary School in the United States.

Did my ears hear correctly? I had to ask my dad to repeat what he just said. Sensing my confusion, my dad quickly kissed my cheek, held my hand in his, and told me that I was going home—not only me, but the entire family. He said to me that we would make it back in time, so I could walk with my eighth-grade class for graduation. Oh my God, it was honestly going to happen! All my dreams were coming true. How do you ever thank a man, my dad, for making all the sacrifices that he did for his family? Once again, he was my hero!

My graduation present from my parents was the news that we were heading back to the USA in time for me to walk in procession with my longtime friends and classmates. It was so much more than I could ever have hoped for. Our emotions were high. We were all anxious to return home; but for me, it meant so much more. What a selfless act of love.

Chapter 6

HEADING HOME

It's a funny thing that coming home looks
the same, smells the same, and feels the
same. You'll realize what's changed *is* you.
—F. Scott Fitzgerald

Preparing to leave Egypt was now a reality. The experiences there were life changing. Looking back to the events over the course of the year has left an impact on me that I believe has helped to form the person that I am today. Learning about and respecting different cultures; understanding how kids, no matter where they come from, are still kids, like me; and how kindness is the key to breaking down all barriers couldn't be learned from a textbook. Real-life experiences were the best teachers as well as the most memorable.

It was a busy time packing up our belongings, and saying good-bye. Emotions were strong. We were excited to know that the time had finally arrived when we were homeward bound. Our family and friends were eager to see us again, and we felt the same. But now that it was happening, and we were leaving, it was difficult to leave behind our friends that we made in Egypt and especially our friend and housekeeper, Sala. He had been our link in this different world that we occupied for over a year. He was the one who kept us safe and protected and made our stay both enjoyable and enlightening.

Poor Sala! He was heartbroken to bid us farewell. He began to look at our family as his family, and he had a good life with us. We treated him with respect and love, and now we were leaving. It had to be hard on him. He couldn't understand how we could take home my cat, Sambo, and leave him behind. Sala told us that he wished that he was my cat so that he could come back with us. Believe me, if we could have brought him home, we would have. He was a wonderful man, but Egypt was his home. It just couldn't be; and so with heavy hearts, we said goodbye and departed for the ship.

I didn't feel as upset saying goodbye to my classmates at CAC because many of them were heading back home too. In fact, if we had stayed longer, I would have had to make new friends, since my old friends were also leaving. We exchanged addresses and phone numbers to keep in touch, and today, I still keep in contact with two very dear friends from Cairo American College over fifty years ago.

We would be traveling home via two cruise ships. The first was on the *Adriatica*, which was waiting for us to join its passengers on the beautiful Mediterranean Sea in Alexandria. The water was something that I had never seen before. It was crystal clear that you could see your feet planted in the sandy bottom. The varied shades of blue reminded me of a painter's pallet. We departed from Alexandria and arrived in Naples where the SS *Constitution* was awaiting our arrival.

The S.S. *Constitution*, which was a Trans-Atlantic Ocean liner, was built to accommodate about a thousand or more passengers. This ship was part of the American Export Lines, and it was taking us back home! The thought of being on this ocean liner was exciting, especially after the experiences that my mother, brother, and I had on our flight overseas. Flying was simply not an option. The sound of going home by a cruise ship was exciting. Better yet, we'd be able to walk around and not be confined to our seats as we were on the flight over.

Our ship was magnificent not only in size but in beauty as well. The vessel had an elegance about her, regal and majestic with her sleek lines—nothing splashy, just classy. Two tall smokestacks stood high above the ocean liner, almost reaching to the sky. This long white vessel with the American flag waving on the bow seemed to be inviting her prospective guest to come aboard. Proudly etched on the front of the ship was the ship's name with what appeared to be gold lettering. The docks were buzzing with activity. The crew was busy gathering the luggage from the passengers and loading supplies on board for our departure. Families were hugging and saying their goodbyes. It was a busy place filled with much activity and emotions. I was eager to get on board. My brother was running back and forth on the dock, being nosy, checking out the crew members and what they were doing, trying to understand just how the ocean liner was able to be tied to the dock, and growing more impatient by the minute to set sail.

Finally (what seemed to be hours), we were invited on board. Walking up the gangway, I glanced down at the water below and felt a bit seasick, and we hadn't gotten underway yet. Although the water was calm and beautiful shades of blue, I knew how rocky this trip could get once we were out in the vast ocean. The water slapped against the sides of the dock, causing tiny white waves to form. The engines also created a ruffle in the water, and it became all too clear at that exact moment just how rough being out to sea could be. Glancing upward, seeing the lifeboats suspended on the sides of the ship had me pause momentarily to say a prayer or two that this trip would be uneventful (weather wise) and smooth sailing. My mother sensed my hesitation as we continued walking up the gangway and grabbed my hand, telling me not to worry and that everything would be fine. These words seemed all too familiar, like when we were flying on the 747 jet to Egypt.

Once on board, it reminded me of a floating hotel. The hallways were narrow and neatly lined with carpet. The decks were clean and well cared for, with comfortable chairs neatly arranged, some with umbrellas to shelter its guests from the intense sun. Some areas had been set up for playing shuffle board and ping-pong. There was a library to take out books to read as you sat by the pool. This was something the adults took advantage of more than the kids.

As we continued with the tour, we turned the corner, and when my brother and I laid our eyes on the Olympic-size pool, we knew that this would be our hangout. Continuing with our tour, we stopped in the dining area, which was elegant and warmly lit. The crew was busy preparing for our first meal once we were underway. The arrangement of fruits and delicious foods looked more like an artist arranged each piece than the chef. Being at sea was making me hungry. There was a band in the dining area tuning up their instruments, so I could only imagine that meant that music would serenade us as we dined this evening. It was an unbelievable experience. They thought of everything to make this voyage enjoyable for young and old alike.

Leaving the dining area, we were shown to our cabins. Although my cabin, #P 63, was small in comparison to my bedroom at home, it was not cramped. The closet space was small, about a foot wide. I wondered how I was going to fit all my stuff into this tiny closet. It looks like a lot will be staying in my luggage. It really doesn't matter since I plan on spending most of my time poolside. Seeing the neatly hung curtains, I decided to take a peek out the porthole. The water was calm now, but once I was told by a crew member that there are times while at sea when the water can be rough, causing the water to swell, I decided it was just best to leave the curtains closed. It was better that way.

As we were getting ready to settle in and unpack our things, the ship's whistle blew, and the crew member told us that it meant it was midday at sea (noon). I am glad I was prewarned, as hearing that whistle without understanding its meaning would have set my mind into thinking something was wrong.

A voice came over the intercom from our captain. He introduced himself to the passengers. Captain Charles E. Reilly invited us on this fantastic voyage. He suggested that we head for the deck to wave our goodbyes to those on the dock as we prepared to leave Naples and begin our homeward voyage. Of course, my brother and I headed immediately for the deck and held on as the anchor was pulled, ropes untied, and our ship pulled out for the mighty seas. Farther out into the vast ocean, while on deck, my brother and I took notice of sharks circling near the ship. I couldn't believe what we were witnessing. I was happy to be looking down at them from high above instead of being on a smaller vessel. I guess they were looking for scraps from the kitchen. All I know is I was happy when they disappeared from my view.

How could such a large vessel travel at such speeds and stay afloat? I couldn't wrap my mind around this concept, and for me, it was just part of the magic that I was feeling, sailing on this luxury ocean liner. I wasn't much concerned about the scientific reasons that made this possible; I just wanted to continue on with my magical ride. I found my utopia! I just knew that I wouldn't mind how long this trip was going to take. There was no comparison to the long, tedious flight that brought us overseas. Sailing was the way to travel!

My magical trip began. I soon learned that I walked on the same deck that several famous people walked, such as Lucille Ball and Desi Arnaz for their show *Bon Voyage* back in 1955, Grace Kelly when she took her voyage on this ship to marry her prince in Monaco back in 1956, and then Gary Grant and Deborah Kerr in their movie *An Affair to Remember* back in 1957. I liked living this part of history. I just knew that this was going to be a magical voyage; look at its history!

There was so much to do on the ship, but pulling into port had its own share of excitement. Visiting places in history and seeing them firsthand was better than simply reading about them. I learned this in Egypt when I took a camel ride through the Sahara Desert and witnessed the splendor of the magnificent Pyramids or stood by the

Sphinx, which is a massive statue of a lion with the face of a pharaoh believed to stand guard at Giza to protect the pyramid. I stood by the colossal statue of Ramsey in downtown Cairo and rode on a boat down the Nile River.

Nothing compares to actually seeing these sights in person. Being able to go back in time, entering the majestic Pyramids, and reverently standing in the room where ancient pharaohs prepared for their final journey to the hereafter has been forever etched in my memory. Reading a textbook or watching an educational documentary on these magnificent wonders somehow did not capture the same emotions that seeing them in person did. I stood where great kings and queens once lived. History was alive here, made here, and here I walked.

I marvel at how these Egyptians were able to build such massive and timeless works of art (pyramids) by hand. I will always remember as I reflect back on those special moments when I was privileged to walk back in time, moving from chamber to chamber.

Being able to visit so many ancient places along the way and staying in port for a few days to actually get the opportunity to take tours and learn more about other lands and their history was both educational as well as impressive. Naples, Italy, was one adventure that still remains with me today. The devastation that the eruption of Mt. Vesuvius caused to the people in Pompeii was haunting. The sight of the twisted bodies of men, women, children, and animals frozen in time as they ran for safety, huddled together, lying on the floor face down, overcome from the lava or ashes, is etched in my memory forever. Over 16,000 innocent people lost their lives that day, and what is even scarier is the fact that this volcano is still active.

Strolling down the cobblestone streets that once were alive with so much activity was a sad reminder of how time has changed everything. Peering out at Mt. Vesuvius, tranquil for now, was a sad reminder of how quickly lives were lost and everything changed on that day. What struck me as odd was how towering columns of stone sustained this devastation when the rest of the building was gone, crumbled to the ground. There are some things that remain in your memory no matter what your age when you first see them.

Stopping in Rome held both sadness and joy. To have walked where so many gladiators gave their lives, where chariots travelled, and lions roared while spectators—fifty to eighty thousand of them—cheered and witnessed this gruesome sport made me glad that I didn't live back in those days. Amazingly, though, the Colosseum, circular and robust, built over two thousand years ago, stands for the most part still today.

I had a sick feeling when I entered the arched openings in this historical building. As I glanced upward to the tiered seating, where so many spectators sat to watch the events unfold, and walked in and out of the underground rooms that housed humans and animals, a strange feeling overcame me. I couldn't help but reflect on this time in history and ponder over the fact that so many valiant gladiators fearlessly entered and fought to their death right there where I was standing. Walking the same grounds like so many brave people walked so long ago and where many lost their lives was both sad and eerie. My brother loved visiting the Colosseum; however, I felt the opposite emotion and was happy to exit both this time and place in history.

Touring the Vatican and the Trevi Fountain was delightful. My family was fortunate to have had an audience with Pope John XXIII as well as tour the beauty of the Sistine Chapel. Michelangelo's artwork is magnificent! What talent and grace surrounded this chapel! Being fortunate to take in all this beauty was breathtaking. No matter what your religious beliefs, no one can deny the beauty that surrounds this area.

The Trevi Fountain was such a tranquil and beautiful place to visit. This public fountain—filled with crowds taking in its beauty, listening to the calming sounds of the water as it trickled down from the various statues seated high above—was mesmerizing. Everyone was making wishes as they tossed their coins into the fountain. I was becoming anxious as well as impatient for my turn to approach the fountain.

Legend has it that you need to toss your coin or coins in a specific way. You are supposed to take your coin in your right hand, place it over your left shoulder with your back to the fountain, and toss it, making your wish. Legend says if you toss one coin into the fountain, you will return, two coins and you will find a new romance, three coins and you will either be married or divorce (whichever it is that you are hoping for). After my third coin was tossed into the fountain, I turned around to face the fountain again and reflect on its magic when, much to my surprise, I was pinched on the buttocks. What a shock that was for me, especially since I was not looking for a husband yet! I was flattered by this gesture; however, after my father heard what just happened, his feelings were not like mine! Things happen quickly in Rome!

So many breathtaking sights, as well as rich experiences both in Egypt and on the trip home, I have been fortunate enough to enjoy and realize that this was a once-in-a-lifetime opportunity.

Back on the ship, the food continued to flow, more delicious than the day before. Each meal was prepared with such detail and exquisite taste. The dining area had fine linens, china, crystal stemware, colorful floral arrangements, and ice sculptures as you entered. My favorite part of the dinner was always the huge dessert table that was filled with every kind of dessert imaginable.

A new decorative menu graced the table each morning with a wide variety of meals to choose from, one better than the next. These menus were unique and not like the ones you find in a restaurant at home, same menu every day. They had various artistic designs on the cover, suitable for framing, with each day presenting a different artist's works. We dined at the captain's table, which was an honor. Everyone dressed up, men in suits and ties and ladies in dresses. The orchestra played as we ate, and once everyone was finished eating, the music changed from soft dinner music to partying music. This was my brother and my cue to exit the dining room, return to our cabins, and get changed back into our bathing suits and head for the pool. We let the adults remain in the dining area to dance the night away.

There was a program of events listed daily, one for the kids and one for the adults. The crew made sure that everyone's day was filled from sunrise to sunset.

We were nearing the end of this perfect voyage when the tides changed, and the ocean decided to show us just how rough she could be. A severe storm was in the area; skies were dark and cloudy; winds were blowing, causing the flags to rustle; and the once-tranquil ship that I had grown to love began rocking back and forth. The guests in the swimming pool were directed to clear out of the pool immediately, and those on deck were told to go back to their cabins.

My brother and I were in the pool along with some other kids when the water began slapping the sides of the swimming pool with such force that we knew we had to get out fast. Water underneath the ship was tossing, getting stronger and stronger; white caps were forming and gaining in strength as well as in height; and the pool water was now splashing all over the deck. Our parents ran to the deck when they noticed how rough the seas were to get my brother and me to safety.

Once out of the pool, we were directed by the staff to report directly to our cabins. That wasn't a problem for me. All I wanted to do was get into my bed and stay there as I was beginning to feel nauseous from all the rocking. Running through the hallways to enter the cabin was quite a sight. People were getting sick; buckets were available for those who couldn't make it to the bathroom; and some were sitting on the floor with their heads between their legs, while others were stumbling to get to their rooms.

Pushing past the passengers, my brother and I headed for our cabins and flopped down on the bed. Everything—and I mean everything—seemed to be rocking and rolling. The room was swirling around, and all I wanted was for it to stop. When the sea was calm, it was beautiful and peaceful, but when it was rough, it was a different story. We just kept rocking back and forth for what seemed like hours. There was no way that I was going to open my curtains to look outside and see what was going on. I could only imagine how the ocean was swirling around outside my window, and that was reason enough not to peek.

When the storm was over, no one was interested in dining. It was a quiet night on board with soup and crackers. Morning came, and the look on the passengers' faces was quite different from the night before. The passengers were more reserved than usual after the storm and chose to eat a light breakfast of tea and toast. It took some time before everyone was back to wanting to check out the menu and resume feasting on the ship's excellent cuisine.

Thank heavens the stormy weather had passed. The remainder of the voyage was pleasant and uneventful. The last night at sea, Sunday, May 27, 1962, the captain had a farewell dinner for the passengers. It was a black-tie event. There was dancing, laughing, sharing our experiences with one another, and enjoying a show. After dinner, the kids were taken to their own farewell celebrations with the ship's crew. Our cocktail hour was the Coca-Cola cocktail hour, followed by a party designed just for us.

Monday, May 28th was the day I caught a glimpse of the beautiful Statue of Liberty. We had arrived in New York. The excitement was everywhere. Looking out in the distance and catching a glimpse of the Statue of Liberty as she welcomed us home was the most beautiful sight that I have ever seen or will ever see. I was finally home! The emotions that the view of her generated for me was something I have never felt before. I felt somewhat connected to my great-grandmother and how she must have felt when the Statue of Liberty welcomed her and her children into the country so many years ago.

Seeing this Statue of Liberty let me know that I was home and that I was in the most beautiful country in the world, where everything would be okay again.

I couldn't wait to exit the ship. It had been a fabulous journey, one that I will always be grateful for having had, but it now ended, and a new one was about to begin. I was ready for my next adventure.

I didn't walk down the gangway the same way that I entered it back in Alexandria, Egypt. I ran, my feet barely touching the ground. As soon as I was on the ground, I knelt down and kissed it. I was home, back in the United States of America! What a wonderful feeling being back on American soil. No one can fully understand that feeling unless you've been away from home in a foreign land. America is a beautiful place, and it is home!

Peering across the crowd of people anxiously waiting to hug and kiss their loved ones, searching for familiar faces (such as my Nanny and Pop Pop), hearing everyone speaking English, listening to familiar music that I understood told me that I was really home; it wasn't a dream. America the beautiful, how I missed you!

The drive home was a noisy one; everyone had so much to say, so many memories to share. As soon as there was a brief moment of silence, I jumped right in and started right back up with all the chattering. Manners went out the window on the ride home. The rule "wait until the speaker is finished speaking" would never have made it on this ride home. If you took a breath, someone else was taking your spot and talking. Happy memories, happy times—we were all together once again. A new page in our lives was beginning.

Years later, I continued to check on the SS *Constitution*'s whereabouts. I learned that in 1997, while being towed to be scrapped, she sank seven hundred miles north of Hawaii. A historian named Reuben Goossens commented that "it seemed a better end for this fine ship than hundreds of blowtorches cutting her up." I have to agree with him, as she was so majestic. Now, she rests at the bottom of the Pacific Ocean where she proudly travelled so many times and brought so much joy to so many people. Her story began June 25, 1951 and ended November 17, 1997, and I was a piece—a small portion—of that journey!

Chapter 7

A NEW EXPERIENCE—
HIGH SCHOOL

We can only be what we give
ourselves the power to be.
—Native American Proverb

A freshman at last! The hallways seemed endless, the building so crowded with noisy teenage girls rushing from one class to another, faculty at every turn, and not a single boy anywhere—I was in an all-girls school. Classrooms appeared barren compared to the warm, fuzzy, and colorful rooms that I had grown accustomed to in elementary school.

My mind was wandering with thoughts about growing up and how great it was supposed to be, but honestly, walking in these halls, I started to think that growing up may not be all that it was cracked up to be. So many girls pushing through the noisy halls as the bell rang to make it to class on time was somewhat intimidating. It reminded me of the horse races, where the starter gun was fired, and out of the stalls, the horses charged. There was no room for indecision; you had to know in which direction your next class was, or you would be left in the dust. These grounds were unfamiliar and quite daunting.

Sitting in class, looking around at all the new faces, recognizing only a mere few caused my heart to race, my palms to sweat, and fear took over. I wasn't so sure that these unfamiliar grounds were where

I really wanted to be. As the bell rang, class started, and my life as a teenager took off.

Taking the time to reflect on this new experience, I thought in some ways going to an all-girls school might be therapeutic. There were no boys to impress, no fear of rejection, and my only competition was academic. I knew that I was entering high school quite differently than my peers. I saw so much of the world, which had a profound impact on me. I was a teenager where my life lessons broadened my thinking and opened my mind, so much so that what seemed relevant to some of my friends was trivial to me after living abroad. I felt more mature than many of my friends, and I hoped that I could fit into this new phase of my life.

The conversations were different too. Even though the language was English, it was unfamiliar, much like when I landed in Egypt. Now it was all about boys, dating, and how they looked. I, on the other hand, didn't have a boyfriend to talk about, which left me feeling somewhat out of the loop, not a part of the so-called "in crowd." Could my life as a teenager get any worse? I certainly hope not.

As the weeks passed and I became more familiar with my surroundings, I found my way and developed new friendships. Wearing uniforms, where we all looked alike, was comforting. There were some attractive girls in my class, which made me feel all the more out of place. I was tall and quite skinny with minimal curves. I used to be proud of my height, and I carried myself well until I was ridiculed by a teacher who shattered my confidence and made me self-conscious. I was still tall and slender as my years in high school continued, but at least now there were some noticeable curves in places where they should be.

I was beginning to feel better about myself, and my confidence was beginning to surface when a teacher in my junior year decided, for whatever reason she had, to do her best to make me feel inferior. She continued on her mission of tearing down my self-esteem, calling me the "Jolly Green Giant," placing me in the back of the line, making comments that girls shouldn't be as tall as I was (I was 5'8"), and making daily jokes about being so tall. I took this abuse day in and day out, reminding myself that I was only in her class for one subject of this torturous day, and then I was free. Her cruel remarks went on for a full year, and although there were many joyous moments that year, this treatment still haunts me today. What this one person did to me is inexcusable. I once was a young girl, proud to be tall and slender, and today I am a woman who continually thinks about my height when standing next to people, often slouching or refusing to wear heels that add more inches to my height.

Our gym classes were another practice in humility. Our burgundy gym suits were hideous and I believe designed to humble us all. They were a one-size-fits-all one-piece suit. This outfit was unflattering for even the best of shapes. It didn't matter how attractive you were; once you put this suit on, your beauty vanished. If any of us thought that we were attractive, sexy, well portioned, this outfit put that thought to rest. No wonder so many girls came to gym class unprepared. It was worth the detention not to wear the gym suit. Honestly, we all looked like a sack of potatoes as we piled into the gym.

To add insult to injury, on warm sunny days, we marched across the street, which was heavily travelled, into the neighborhood playground to do our warm ups. Truck drivers travelled down this road on a regular basis and they would honk their horns, calling out to us as we continued to do our exercises. Cool guys yelled out the windows of their cars, laughing and pointing. I prayed that the traffic light remained green so they didn't have to stop and have a few additional minutes to peer and hackle at us. We certainly put a smile on many faces and gave them something to talk about when they reached their destinations. Rainy days are not a favorite of mine, but on gym days, they were a blessing. These memories remain with me still to this day, and whenever I pass by my alma mater, I inevitably glance across the street to that famous playground, and I blush with embarrassment from so many years ago.

Sitting in Social Studies class, listening to the instructor talk about places that I had experienced firsthand was just another one of those exciting and memorable experiences in my life. We were learning about countries that I was fortunate enough to have lived in or travelled to when I was in eighth grade. While many of my high school classmates were absorbed in their little worlds, I was not. I saw the world through different lenses as I got to know the people from these lands, their families, their customs, and their unique views on America. I walked where others in my class hadn't. I was able to walk where history took place and learned firsthand, not from textbooks, but from my life experiences. I know how beautiful it is to be an American and to have the freedoms that we have.

In some ways, these experiences gave me an upper hand in class. I felt that I was out of the loop with many of my classmates. Our interests and experiences were on different levels. I had the chance to travel back in time, walking where history was made and not merely turning the pages in a book and reading about them. I lived it, and these were invaluable treasures that were mine, thanks to my father. Just like my classmates at Cairo American College were richer in their knowledge of various languages than I, I now was richer than my classmates through the many experiences I had from my travels.

I recall that terrible day when the news that President John F. Kennedy was assassinated came over the intercom at school. Everyone was in shock. Teachers and students alike were crying in total disbelief. No one could focus on anything else that day as we were all so distraught. I thought back when I saw him when he was campaigning, driving down the street, and waving to all his supporters. It seemed so surreal now that he was gone. He was so young and filled with such promise for America. When I got home from school, I was glued to the television, still not believing what I was hearing. Never in my lifetime did I ever think that a president could or would be killed. It was something that should have been in history books from earlier days and certainly not something that happened now. The whole world was in shock. Unfortunately, this was a part of history, and it was in my lifetime.

During my high school years, I volunteered at the local hospital, working on the pediatric floor. I lived close enough to the hospital that I could walk there if I needed to, but that rarely happened as someone in the family always was available to drive me back and forth. Two career paths that I thought about were becoming a pediatrician or a teacher. Working in the hospital was a great way to find out if this was the avenue that I would pursue upon graduation. I loved being around the children, reading to them and playing board games with them.

During this time, I grew very fond of a little girl who reminded me of a china doll—she was that beautiful. We took a liking to each other, and she'd be waiting for me as I got off the elevator. We liked talking to each other, sharing memories of our times at the shore, and playing games. The nursing staff knew that I was close to her, as did her parents. I would check up on her even on my days off.

One day, as I got off the elevator and headed in the direction of her room, I noticed the nurses' faces as I passed their station. They weren't their cheery selves, so I sensed something had happened. I continued walking to her room and noticed she wasn't there. The room was freshly cleaned, with new bed linens and towels. Something was wrong. I sensed it in the pit of my stomach. I immediately made my way to the nurses' station, and one of the nurses, whom I was quite fond of, took me aside to say that she passed away that morning and that her parents wanted me to know how thankful they were for all the time that I spent with their daughter. She had leukemia, and there was nothing more that could be done for her.

I felt like the floor gave way underneath my feet. I cried and cried and couldn't believe or accept the news that this sweet, innocent little girl was gone. I left the hospital that day and could not get this child out of my mind. Her loss was more than I could bear, and when I saw our family doctor, who also was a dear friend, I poured my heart out to him. He told me to look at this as a sign that I should not be a pediatrician since I took her death so hard and that my calling was more in line with being a teacher. I guess he knew what he was talking about because I gave up this dream and chose the path of teaching instead.

Finally, it was my senior year! So much happening this year: the senior prom, preparing for graduation, senior trip, deciding on which college to attend for teaching, and finally graduating!

As the time began to approach for my prom and the pressure of deciding who I would ask to accompany me, the stress began to surface. I wasn't dating anyone, so whom would I ask? My mother and Nanny (my grandmother), were not going to allow this event to pass by without my attending, telling me how these memories were a part of my high school years, which led to more tension because not only did I not have a date, I now had family telling me that I had to go. Whom would I ask? Who would accept my invitation and not further humiliate me by turning me down? What a dilemma.

As my friends purchased their prom tickets and began shopping for their gowns, I felt even more pressured. As I tossed and turned over whom I could ask, it came to me! I had been friends with my neighbor's son, who was a bit older than I, not really that much older, but older just the same. He was good-looking, fun-to-be-around type of guy, and no threat at all since he looked at me like a sister, and I looked at him like my older brother! That's it! I figured whom I would ask. Now I needed to drum up the courage to ask him to please do me a favor and escort me to my senior prom. How humiliating, but with all the pressure I was getting from home and my friends, I just had to ask.

When I asked him, he happily accepted and was quite the gentleman, understanding that I wanted to go to my prom and that I was in a pickle, since I wasn't dating anyone. Oddly enough, he was happy to experience going to my prom since he had missed out on his own.

Shopping for my gown was thrilling. My mother and Nanny were like high school girls themselves. We went from boutique to boutique, searching for the perfect gown. I tried on so many beautiful gowns—red, pink, blue, purple, and then I found it: emerald green. I felt like Cinderella with this gown. It fit like a glove and accentuated all the right areas. It was magical, this transformation that took place inside me. I no longer cared that it was a friend of mine who was taking me to the prom. I was going, and that was all that mattered.

The night of the prom came, and flashes were going off in every direction in our living room as my father proudly took pictures to capture this special event. My date looked handsome, and when he gave me my wrist corsage, which happened to match my gown perfectly, I became all choked up. These were the first flowers that I received from a man other than my father. As he placed my corsage on my wrist, I wondered how he was able to get them to be such a perfect match, and then I knew. I glanced up at my mother, our eyes met, and that twinkle in her eyes told me that she was the one to make sure these flowers were perfect for her little girl.

My best friend and her boyfriend met us at my house, where the pictures continued. You could feel the difference—or at least I could—between us as couples. Those two were lovebirds, and my date and I were merely friends. I longed for the day when I too would meet someone and feel that connection as they did.

It was a night to remember and one that I am grateful that my mother and Nanny pushed me into attending. Every girl should have a guy friend to rely on in an emergency. He was mine, and he was terrific. I never let the cat out of the bag at the prom that we were just friends. Everyone thought that we were a couple, and that was just fine with me! I finally fit in with the "in crowd."

After the prom and experiencing such a delightful evening, having someone by my side made me dream about one day finding my own Prince Charming. I knew I would know him as soon as I saw him, but when would that be? Where would that be? For now, Prince Charming would remain in my nightly dreams.

Our senior year continued with all the festivities and preparations for the big day when we would graduate and set forth on whatever career paths we each chose. During that time, something unexpected and new came my way. My Nanny had a sister who lived nearby, and she called her to ask her if I would go out on a blind date with a young man who was her neighbor. They had moved to Pennsylvania from New Hampshire, and she thought it would be good if he and I went out. She felt that we would click and be good for one another.

As the conversation continued between the two sisters (my Nanny and my Aunt) the topic of his upcoming senior prom came up and how his mother wanted him to experience happy memories from his high school years, just as my mother had wanted for me. He had recently lost his father and was quite distraught over his death. My aunt, along with his mother, thought they could help ease some of this pain by having him go out more and have some fun with people his age. And now I enter the picture! The matchmakers were my aunt, his mother, and of course my Nanny. Now these women had a tremendous job to do: not only convince him to ask me out on a date but to get me to say yes. They were up for the challenge, but were the two of us?

The task by these matchmakers was to sway this young man into taking a chance with me and going on a date. Phone numbers were exchanged with the stage set. His mother kept pushing on her end for him to call, and Nanny was working on my end to accept the call. The day came when I received the call, and after we chatted for a while, I accepted a date to attend the play *If* by Rudyard Kipling, which he was required to see to gain extra credit points in his English class. It was an awkward situation because neither one of us knew what the other person looked like, what our likes and/ or dislikes were, and if we would really enjoy each other's company; hence, the name "blind date."

The day arrived when I was finally going to meet my date. The butterflies fluttered in my stomach as I tried on one outfit after another in preparation for this date. Nothing seemed to look right: slacks, dress, skirt, and blouse, and then I found it—my gray tweed jumper with the turtleneck was just the ticket! My hair fell into place as it should, and my jumper showed enough of my curves but not too much. I worked on my makeup and was ready to meet Mr. Right.

As I was finishing up with the final touches, my parents announced that he was here. He stood there in my living room, greeted me with a warm smile, and looked as nervous as I felt. Introductions were made, small talk with my parents exchanged, and it was finally time to head out to the play. Outside waiting for us was his black 1963 Chevy 2. He, being the gentleman that he was, opened the passenger door for me; waved goodbye to my parents, who of course were watching from the window; and headed off for a day of getting to know one another.

Conversation flowed easily as we headed for the show, and it felt like we knew each other all our lives. The English assignment was to see the play, which we did. The hundred-dollar question you might ask is what the play was about, to which my reply would be, "I really couldn't begin to tell you." I was wrapped up in studying this fine specimen of a man—how his smile lights up his whole face and made his eyes twinkle, his sense of humor (or was it just nerves), how his laughter was like music to my ears, and how soothing it was to listen to him humming a song on the radio. When we arrived at the house he thanked me repeatedly for helping him get the extra credit in English that he desperately needed to pass the course. I meanwhile was thankful he needed the extra points because it led to many other dates.

It appeared that the matchmakers knew what they were doing when they set us out on our first date. The dates that followed that year held so much fun, laughter, and memories. We were never lost for words or places to go. Being teenagers, we spent many Friday nights bowling, at the movies, and going out to fast-food places to eat. I had a curfew, which was eleven o'clock—and how that time flew. When you are happy and having fun, time seems to get away from you, and before you know it, it is time to head home. So many times, I had wished that my curfew was later, much later; but be that as it may, I respected my parents' rules, and we were always home in time.

I always found it to be funny how my brother, who was younger, would always get a pass when it came to coming in the door late from a date. Mom had different rules for him because her thinking was that he was a boy and could take care of himself. I too was with a boy who could take care of any situation that might arise, just like my brother was with his date, but there was no convincing my mother that her logic made absolutely no sense back then, nor does it make sense today. My mother was firm in her decision, and there was no arguing with her.

His prom was quickly approaching, and he asked me to go. *Wow*, my whole world was changing. I was being asked to go to a prom with a guy who really cared about me. I had a real boyfriend. What a difference this prom would be in comparison to mine. Of course, my answer was "Yes" without any hesitation.

It was early spring, and the night of the prom was here. I chose to wear my emerald green gown once again with all the accessories. I looked at other gowns, but none could compare to the one I already owned. It was as if the designer had me in mind. The lines in this gown were exquisite, empire bust, straight with a slit down the side. This was the gown that showed off my girly shape and made me look like I was a model. I longed for him to see me in this gown and couldn't wait to see his reaction when I entered the room. I felt beautiful and hoped he felt the same way. If you believe in fairy tales, then this was my fairy tale, my Cinderella moment.

When I entered the room, our eyes met, and I knew by the expression on his face that I chose the right evening gown for this night. Everything was perfect that evening. It was as if I was the princess, and he was my prince. Words need not be uttered at that moment, for his face said it all. I felt loved for the first time, and it was magical. He took my hand into his as we departed for an enchanted evening. Every slow dance that we danced, I felt like he could feel my pounding heart and know just what was going through my mind. As I rested my head on his shoulder, the smell from his cologne was delicious and so tempting. I wanted to stop the clock and let this night, this feeling, go on forever. If this is what love felt like, then I knew at that very moment, I was truly in love with this man.

I believe that evening was the start of our future together. We spent every moment that we could with each other. Our families were close too, which made for happy times. Family, neighbors, and friends enjoyed Friday evenings at my parents' home around the picnic table that my dad had built. The laughter and stories shared by all were heartwarming. Friday nights meant pizzas, steak sandwiches, and hoagies. Everyone looked forward to gathering here each weekend, and our curfew was soon forgotten or overlooked, which gave us an extra half hour or hour.

It's funny how falling in love can change everything. I felt alive, happy, and eager to face each day. Weekends were filled with the unexpected. We would jump into the car, fill up the tank, and ride with no particular place in mind, ending up at some of the most wonderful places. One Sunday, we went to Valley Forge, and as we were walking up and down the steep hills, this quiet, reserved girl, turned into someone very playful and quite mischievous, darting up and down the hills, chasing after each other, laughing as I kicked off my heels and tore my pantyhose, running with the breeze following my every move. I was like a deer, free and wild, and it was wonderful.

When he finally caught up to me (of course I let him), the capture was spectacular. Grabbing me in his arms, placing his warm lips on mine, falling to the ground, and being lost in the moment was pure heaven. This was love, cherishing the unexpected moments and being swept away in them! I read these words somewhere, and they best describe how I was feeling that day: "Sing, like no one is listening. Dance, like there is no one watching. Love, like you've never been hurt. And Live, like it's your last day on earth." Moments like these should never be few and far between; they should be at the soul of everything you do, to live life to the fullest.

Picnics at Washington Crossing with both families; trips to Ocean City, New Jersey, for special moments at the beach; endless walks early in the morning along the beach; trips to New Hampshire; and enjoying concerts were all times that brought both families together to celebrate happy times.

Graduation Day was here; after twelve long years, the moment arrived, and my emotions ran wild. I was excited yet apprehensive about leaving. These walls kept me safe, I had a daily routine, and someone was always guiding me in the right direction. Now the decisions were mine.

The friendships I developed with these girls would, quite honestly, for the most part, be a fleeting memory. I knew I wouldn't see most of them after today. I had a few close friends, but even with that, our goals and career plans were going in different directions. Maybe I was thinking too deeply about graduation and what it meant, but it was a reality.

As we were securing our caps with lots of bobby pins, making sure they didn't fall off, we hurried to line up as the graduation pomp and circumstances began. It was at this very moment when the realization struck me that I was leaving my childhood behind and was about to enter into a whole new world—adulthood.

Families were calling out their loved ones' names, cheers were echoing as each one's name was called and their diploma issued. The excitement from the crowds was contagious. It was a happy place to be.

As we exited the auditorium, there waiting for me was my remarkable family and my love, with a dozen roses. One of my closest friends came over, and we had pictures taken together. We went through all our schooling together, and now we were headed down different paths. While chatting, she commented on how I wouldn't have to deal with all the teasing and "tall jokes" any longer. She mentioned that she didn't know how I endured the ridicule all these years. My parents overheard our conversation and asked for clarification. Well, as the saying goes, the cat was out of the bag now, and so I proceeded to relive this painful experience, the jokes, and cruel remarks that were made about my height, as well as being called "olive oil," "jolly green giant," and many other hurtful names.

The look on my parent's face was one of sheer shock. They were horrified. They demanded to know why I never told them of this mistreatment because they certainly would have handled it immediately, and it would have ended. Instead, I suffered this abuse for two years. I reminded them of my upbringing where they believed that the teacher was always right, and if I got in trouble by a teacher in school, I'd be in more trouble when I got home. I guess I misunderstood their message and kept this locked deep inside. I felt sorry for them as I watched their expressions as I relayed the story. My parents told me that I should have trusted them with the facts and that I should never have gone through such an ordeal alone. Lesson learned! Somehow, though, I think having gone through this on my own gave me the inner strength that I needed to survive. I was thankful it was over, and I could move on.

Graduation parties were plentiful. Our senior week at the New Jersey shore was awesome. The girls and I hung out at the beach, walked the boards, and relaxed. We weren't real party people, so getting intoxicated was never a concern for our parents. Unfortunately, we did get too much sun one hot day, and we suffered with sun poison for several days after. That happened only once in my lifetime—lesson well learned!

And so with our graduation behind us, we now had to face the next phase of our lives—*adulthood!* I knew what direction I wanted to go, which was teaching. As for Terry, his plans would have to be placed on hold for a while. The draft began back in 1940 and lasted until 1973. It was mandatory for every male upon reaching his eighteenth birthday to enter into the service. Terry had to choose a branch of the service to enter first before he could pursue his dreams. So as exciting as graduation was for me, it had its drawbacks for him.

Chapter 8

ENTERING TWO DIFFERENT WORLDS—WORK AND MILITARY

When life changes to be harder,
change yourself to be stronger.
—Unknown

The work world wasted no time in taking away our carefree moments that were ours right out of high school. I was preparing to become a teacher and was dedicated and determined to be successful both in college as well as in my classroom. Teaching was my passion. I felt confident that I found my profession and eagerly embraced my decision. Terry, on the other hand, went on job interviews and worked for a steel company until it was time to join the US Navy, the summer of 1968, as the Vietnam War was escalating.

In the early days, if you maintained good grades, you were able to enter into teaching in the private school sector without having your certification. You needed your clearances, and you were mandated to continue attending college, working toward your degree. I was fortunate enough to be accepted into this program right out of high school. I attended college at night as well as throughout the summer and taught during the day.

My first assignment was a third-grade classroom. The class size was enormous, over sixty students; today, that size is a thing of the past. I recall the moment I glanced into what would be my classroom, filled with students' desks and thinking to myself, *How will I handle all these young lives?* Before meeting my students, I had some household chores to do before thinking about lesson plans. There was cleaning, decorating, and rearranging furniture and desks. Luckily for me, I had so much help turning my classroom into a place that was warm and welcoming. Family members, my boyfriend, along with our family physician, who was a personal friend, chipped in to make my classroom perfect. My classroom had the special touches of family and friends, and I felt good about these accomplishments. I hoped making the classroom inviting with all the decorations and warmth would help ease the students' minds as well as mine. They weren't the only ones who had the first-day jitters.

The first day of school arrived and what a class I had! I never saw so many children in one room at a time, and I was the one who had the awesome task of teaching each and every one of them. There were no words for what was running through my mind. Meeting my class and hearing about their summer adventures put me at ease and hopefully them as well. I can honestly say that I fell in love that day, and I was more determined to help each and every child succeed. My heart was committed to each child that entered my classroom.

For the most part, my first year went by uneventfully, except for one incident where I had to run after a student who left the school without permission, heading down for the highway. Without hesitation, I notified the office to watch the rest of my class, and off I went after him, high heels and all. I took my heels off so that I could run faster to catch him, which I did. I only wish I had a camera to capture what I looked like at that moment (torn stockings, hair a mess, and sweating). What a sight that must have been! I always prided myself in dressing professionally, but that moment, I looked anything but professional. I often laugh about that day. My only concern that day at that moment was to keep my student safe, and that I did. Nothing else mattered until I looked at myself and realized I needed to catch the train home after school.

My parents worried about my getting home later in the evening, taking the train, and being at the train station alone, and so they helped me purchase a car, which gave not only them some piece of mind, but me as well. With this purchase, I was able to stay at school later because I didn't have to worry about catching a train anymore. I now operated on my schedule from then on and not the train's schedule.

Fast forward many, many years later, when I was seeking employment outside of teaching, when I met a former student of mine from that infamous first class. I left teaching briefly because I married and had children and now needed to have my degree in order to return to teaching. The policy for teaching without your certification was once you left the field, which I did to have my children, you could not reenter without your teaching credentials, which meant graduating from college.

I needed employment while attending college to acquire my degree. I responded to an ad that appeared in the newspaper. As this fine gentleman was interviewing me, I noticed the name on his desk, and I instantly knew who he was. I wondered if he recognized me and doubted that he did since I had a different last name now. Never letting on that I knew him (from third grade, my first class), we continued with the interview, and he offered me the position, which I happily accepted.

Upon arrival to my new job the following day, there on my desk was his third-grade report card along with an apple for his teacher. He remembered! We chuckle and reminisced over that year as well as my leaping into action chasing one of his classmates. I laughed and said after looking over his report card, "Thank God you were an A student!" Life has its twists and turns!

The draft was still in effect, and the war in Vietnam was all that the media reported. Two years after high school, Terry's life was about to change, as was mine. He was called to service in 1968 into the Navy. My heart sank as I worried about his safety and selfishly knew that I would be lost without him by my side. We had grown so close and were beginning to plan our future. How quickly those happy, carefree moments can change in just an instant.

Terry went to Boot Camp in the Great Lakes for three months. It seemed like an eternity for us as we were so accustomed to spending every moment with each other. I wrote every day and cried every night. Upon completion of his training, he had no specific designation. These orders would follow shortly.

The long-awaited time that he was away in Boot Camp was coming to an end, and I was going to see him at last. As he walked toward me, in full uniform, I was struck with how much he had changed. Standing before me, he appeared so mature and, of course, so very handsome in his naval uniform. Everything about him showed a confidence I hadn't seen or noticed before. It was as if he left a boy and returned a man. I ran into his arms; he dropped his duffle bag and hugged me with such passion and strength. It felt good to be in his arms once again. God knows I loved this man. We held hands and continued to sneak a kiss here and there on the way home. I wasn't about to let go of his hand.

Later when we were alone, he surprised me with an engagement ring as he proposed. Need I tell you there was no hesitation in my response? "Yes," I said, "I want to be your wife."

We hoped to marry before he went overseas; however, my parents, and more so my father, had different plans. My father's rule was that "Terry needed to serve at least one year, and if the feelings were the same, then he would give us his blessing." I wasn't happy with that decision, but we honored my father's wishes and celebrated our engagement, knowing that after the year apart, we would still be in love and would begin planning for our wedding.

Our engagement celebration didn't last long as Terry departed for a strange land, alone, and so very young. I shuttered to think how long we'd be apart, worried about him daily, and prayed for him nightly.

Assignments were issued, and he was assigned to the ship *Washtenaw County* LST 1166 as a cook. An LST is a landing ship or tank landing ship, used to support amphibious operations by carrying tanks, vehicles, cargo, and landing troops directly onto shore with no docks or piers.

Terry would meet his ship in Japan and remain there for two years. Like me, Terry would become culturally enriched with the sights that he saw and the people he met in Japan, Korea, China, Philippines, and Hawaii. We both led sheltered lives, but our travels opened our eyes to new sights as well as new cultures.

His ship, the *Washtenaw County* LST 1166, travelled down the Mekong Delta four months at a time. This river was dirty, murky, and chocolate in color with dense jungles on each side filled with Vietcong. The mission was dangerous: watching out for the Vietcong hiding in the jungles, ready to shoot, as well as nightly watches for swimmers coming out to the ship, placing magnetic mines between the pontoons and the ship. No one could relax or let their guard down when you were stationed there. Everyone had to be alert at all times.

On one occasion, after completing his four-month mission, the men were heading back for some R & R (Rest and Relaxation), feeling grateful they survived the mission, when they received a call to return to the Mekong Delta because their sister ship, the *Westchester County* LST had been badly hit. A Vietcong swimmer managed to plant mines below the water line causing massive damage to the vessel as well as taking twenty-six lives. The explosions ripped through the ship, causing extensive damage. The *Washtenaw County* turned around and made its way back down the Mekong Delta. It was stationed there for less than a month when another LST vessel came to relieve them so they could head back.

The ship, the *Washtenaw County* LST 1166 played a huge role in the Vietnam War. This ship had many duties such as carrying ammo, supplies; serving as a landing field for planes, Cobra gun ships, and Hueys, which carried the wounded out and brought in the new troops; as well as feeding the marines and ground troops. This mighty ship served from 1953 to 1973 and was honored with seventeen battle stars, two Presidential Unit Citations, two Navy Unit Commendations, and four Meritorious Unit Commendations for her service in the Vietnam War.

These brave military men were subjected to the harmful effects of Agent Orange, which was an herbicide and defoliant used by the US military as part of its herbicidal warfare program. The purpose was to spray the massively dense jungles and to eliminate the forest cover to North Vietnamese and Vietcong troops as well as the crops that might be used to feed them.

When you have a loved one in the service, listening to the news reports is both scary and stressful. Your mind wanders to where your loved one is, asking questions such as, "Is my loved one okay? Is that the area on the news where he might be?" and so on. It no longer is a matter of listening to the facts reported and then moving about your daily routine. It affects every part of you because your heart is there, miles and miles away from home, with your loved one. When you don't receive a letter for a few days, your thoughts tend to go to the dark side, and when the mailman finally delivers the mail and you recognize the writing on the envelope, you can breathe again. I could usually tell how Terry's day or week went by his letters. When he drew the Peanut's character Snoopy from Charlie Brown on my envelope or in my letter with a cute saying, I knew he had a fairly stress-free week. I looked forward to seeing Snoopy!

War is a terrible thing. It not only affects the person serving in the war, but it hits those at home as well. It has a profound effect on everyone. I wrote to Terry every day; sent cards that expressed my love and devotion to him; and as I lay my head down on my pillow every night, I thanked God for keeping him safe today and begged that He would continue to watch over him.

The war was unpopular in the States, and the Vietnam veterans did not receive the warm welcome they were entitled to receive after serving. They didn't ask to participate in this war; they had no choice. They were victims of the draft, and they should never have been mistreated like they were for serving our country. Seeing protester signs, hearing nasty remarks were not the way these servicemen should have been greeted when they came home from the war. The Vietnam War (1962–1972) was a terrible war, as are all wars, and the military should have had a much better homecoming.

This war took its toll on so many young Americans. Like my father, Terry chose not to talk about the sights and sounds of that war. But unlike my father who served in World War II and was welcomed and cheered when they came home, those who served in Vietnam did not have the same love and support from a nation that they called their home upon their return, which is a sadness that still weighs heavily on many hearts.

Chapter 9

MEET THE NEW MR. AND MRS.

Love is not about how much you
say, "I love you" but how much
you can prove that it's true.

—Unknown

This love of ours grew stronger with time, and we married. Funny
how some things have a way of repeating themselves. My parents were married during my father's service years, and I was now experiencing the same thing. I now understood the pain of separation and the worry that the war would claim my loved one. Times were different, the war had a different name, but the love between husband and wife was the same. I too would travel with my husband.

After serving his first year overseas, Terry flew home for a thirty-day leave, at which time we would be married with our parents' blessings. Life has its ups and downs, and now after being separated for a year, we were going to have some time together again, this time as husband and wife.

While Terry was overseas, I planned our wedding with the help of our parents and Nanny. I wanted our wedding day to be magical, to have everything taken care of so that all he needed to do when he arrived home was to get fitted for his tux. He selected a white tux jacket pipped with a thin black strip with black slacks as we had a summer wedding. Every single detail was taken care of for our special day, leaving him without any of the stressors that come with wedding planning so that he was able to enjoy his time home and away from the war.

Everything was ready for the special day—we had our date for the church; his uncle, who was a monsignor, would be able to marry us in our home church; our reception hall was reserved as well as our food choices and music. Flowers selected for the bridesmaids were white roses with touches of lavender and carnations adorned with long flowing lavender ribbons. My bouquet was cascading white roses, which accented my gown beautifully. My final fitting was complete, and it looked like everything was a go. Now, all that was needed was for our day to arrive—June 28.

My gown was stunning. I had seen it in a bridal magazine and knew at first sight that this was the one. Once I saw it, I knew nothing else would do. I felt like the designer had me in mind when she created it. My wedding gown had sleek lines, a beautiful beaded top, and long sleeves that came to a point at my fingertips. The long train, with scalloped etched edges, flowed gracefully. The train was detachable, making it easier for dancing. The gown was designed to be beautiful with or without the train.

Every girl dreams of her wedding day, looking and feeling like a princess, and I was no different. Although I was nervous and worried that everything would be perfect for our day, I was excited to be entering this phase of our lives. The evening before our wedding, after the dress rehearsal, I checked over my list again to make sure that I left nothing to chance. My mother was doing the same thing with her list, as this day just had to be perfect.

Sleeping was almost impossible that night. So much was racing through my head. Eventually, I dozed off, and then, before I knew it, the alarm went off. The long-awaited day was finally here! I jumped out of bed, checked that my gown was still hanging on the door, and then walked through my house one more time as a single girl, who occupied this space for so many years. I had a funny feeling in the pit of my stomach when I realized this was the last time that I would be here as a single woman. The next time I entered through these doors, I would be a married woman and on my own. This house would always welcome me, but I was now about to venture out on my own and create my own home.

Everyone was rushing around the house, flowers were picked up, hair and makeup were in progress for the ladies, and the house was getting its final makeover before photos were taken. Try as I might to remain calm, the hustle-bustle that was all around me was making this impossible. As I looked in the mirror as my makeup was being applied, I realized that this was the last time that I'd be a single woman; my life was about to change.

Once my wedding gown was on, I knew that this was real, and my day had finally arrived. I couldn't believe that today, I was really going to be married to my high school sweetheart. My brother came into the room and placed a good luck penny in my shoe. I have this penny still to this day! The photographer captured these moments, one snap after another. My dad, having been a photographer himself in his earlier years, and having taken many wedding photos, knew how to set up each pose for the right effect, capturing each moment, leaving nothing to chance. Dad made sure our photographer was on top of every moment. The bridesmaids arrived at the house, along with my future mother-in-law, and the photo session continued. There was a lot of laughter and celebration, and then the time had arrived for us to leave for the church, and our nerves set in.

The weather was on our side, sun shining, not a cloud in the sky or wind blowing, just a picture-perfect day. It was sweltering hot; in fact, it was a record-breaking heat wave, but who was complaining?

What a majestic church to become husband and wife! It was a dream to be saying our wedding vows and promising ourselves to each other in such a gorgeous church. The smooth and polished floors leading up to the altar were marble. High cathedral ceilings surrounded the walls with artistic works that put me back to my days in Rome in the Sistine Chapel. The stained glass windows were illuminated with sunlight shining through, as if the heavens were rejoicing with us. The altar had high marble pillars holding an alabaster canopy, where we would stand and profess our love for each other. In the center, gracefully suspended over the altar, hung a gold crucifix, reminding us of our faith and the blessings that the sacred bonds of Holy Matrimony were about to be bestowed on us.

Walking up the many steps leading to the church's entrance, my nerves set in once again. As the door opened and the bridal party and I stood in the vestibule, we could hear the organist's music and quickly took our positions to proceed down the aisle. The white runner was rolled down the aisle, stopping at the altar, where waiting for me was my husband-to-be. The pews were filled with family and friends, eager to congratulate us and share in our celebration.

As I walked down the long aisle, holding on to my father's arm, we glanced into each other's eyes and sensed what each was feeling. My dad gently tapped my arm and smiled. We continued the walk until we reached the altar. My dad gently took my arm and placed it on Terry's, lifted my veil with tear-filled eyes, and kissed me before returning to his pew, where my mother was seated. I know that at this precise moment, one life ended and a new one began.

Terry and I faced one another as we professed our love and placed our wedding rings on each other's finger. As Monsignor Ed read the marriage verses, particularly the one that stated, "The two shall become one," I felt this all along. I always felt so close to him, so much so that we thought alike, knew what the other was thinking before either of us said it. Having God's blessings, we proudly turned to our family and friends, who were seated before us, as we were introduced for the first time as Mr. and Mrs., hand in hand; we walked—more like danced—down the aisle to greet our guests.

Off to the Doral, a beautiful and exquisite hall, to celebrate and enjoy the festivities. This reception hall complimented the church in its beauty. Suspended from the high ceilings were crystal chandeliers which illuminated a spiral staircase that served for many of our photos. The main ballroom serving two hundred guests was richly decorated with elegant linen tablecloths and napkins, complementing our color theme which was lavender along with floral arrangements in the same color hues. The waiters and waitresses were attentive and eager to serve our guests, making sure they had everything needed.

The music played softly as we dined. Once dinner was through, the music changed and the invitation was extended to our guests to join us on the dance floor. Terry and I had chosen the song "More" as our first dance as husband and wife. We hardly moved during our special dance, as we were locked in each other's embrace sharing kisses and lost in the moment as our song continued to play. We were in awe of each other, our day, and all those who came to celebrate our new beginning.

My dad and I danced to the traditional song "Daddy's Little Girl." As my dad took my hand to lead me onto the dance floor it immediately took me back to when I was a little girl and how he taught me to dance by standing on his shoes. Today, I stood on my own two feet, and gracefully glided across the dance floor with him.

Terry danced with his mother (teary eyed) as they too reflected back to his days as a young boy and the many memories that were theirs and theirs alone. Terry was a smooth dancer; as his mother had him take dancing lessons when he was a young boy. It was beautiful to see the love between a mother and her son, as was the love between a father and his daughter.

After the traditional dances, the dance floor became quite lively. It was apparent that everyone was enjoying themselves. As we stood back and watched our guests, a sense of joy came over us, knowing that this day was perfect, not only for Terry and me, but for everyone who came and joined in our celebration.

As we left the hall and were getting into the car, I turned around and glanced at the doors of the hall. I could still hear the music and the laughter of our guests. As I listened to the festivities, a feeling washed over me like a wave that this was truly the beginning of the first day of the rest of our lives together.

We were off to the Pocono Mountains for our honeymoon where so many young couples spent their first time together as a married couple. Each day held new activities shared with other new-lyweds. We embraced these seven days because we knew that reality would set in, and he would be off once again to serve our country. Every day was a gift, and we planned to live it to the fullest. We didn't want this moment to end.

Chapter 10

OUR SERVICE YEARS
AS A FAMILY

Fill your life with experiences, not things.
Have stories to tell, not stuff to show.
—Unknown

Terry departed to join his ship, the *Washtenaw County* LST 1166 in Japan while I stayed back in Pennsylvania. I would eventually join him but not now. I returned to teaching, and he returned to serving our country.

After serving an additional year overseas, Terry returned home for his leave. After spending time with our family and friends, we departed together for California, where he would join the USS *San Bernardino* LST 1189, and here we would begin our married life together. This ship eventually was sent to Vietnam; fortunately for us, however, Terry's service time was complete before the ship departed, so he was not required to go.

Upon our arrival into Long Beach, California, we stayed at a Holiday Inn and searched through the ads for an apartment. Luckily, we came across an apartment in Signal Hill, California, where the occupants were all Naval families. It was scary being out there on my own because Terry had to remain on board the ship, which meant I was alone until the weekend or his days off. Thankfully, this feeling of being alone didn't last long as the Navy wives in the apartment complex were just like me, and we soon became one happy family.

All the wives were alone until their husbands returned, which made it pleasant. We became close friends and bonded together, helping each other through some of the most challenging times. Lasting friendships developed, friendships that continue to this day.

Shortly after arriving in California, I became pregnant with our first child. My parents were thrilled beyond words, as was my Nanny, since this was to be their first grandchild/great-grandchild. So many miles separated us from one another, making it more difficult at this time. Thank God the friendships that were developed with the ladies in the complex were strong, and we looked out for each other. Ironically, most of the girls were expecting as well, so we had a lot in common. We checked on each other every morning as well as every night before retiring. This kinship was amazing, one that, unfortunately, I never experienced again.

During the early hours one morning, alone and scared, I experienced an earthquake. The furniture in the apartment moved, the bed shimmied across the room, and the picture frames and little knick-knacks moved close to the end of the bureau, some falling off from all the shaking. Things on the counter in the kitchen were crashing to the floor, and there was a lot of banging. I didn't know what was happening at first, and then realizing that this had to be an earthquake, I immediately got out of bed and stood in the archway of the apartment. There, right with me, were all my friends, standing in their entrances of their individual apartments, waiting for this shaking, rocking, and rolling to stop. We were all pregnant, and we were all alone. It was an experience I pray I never have to encounter again.

When things settled down, we went to the ground level to the courtyard and just hugged one another. Outside the complex, part of the street had opened up from the quake, and a car was partially face-down in the hole. As for our spouses, they never knew what we went through as they did not experience the after effects on board their ships. They heard about it on the news and radio, so they checked on us, but they had no idea the panic that went through each one of us that morning. As we reflected back on that frightful morning, we turned a bad situation into one where we could laugh. We laughed thinking about five pregnant women standing in their doorways, and what a sight that must have been. This would have been a Kodak moment!

Some good news followed after that ordeal. I was given a surprise baby shower via the phone. My mother and dear neighbor had a baby shower where all my family and friends gathered and celebrated. They took pictures of my shower and had all the gifts sent to us. A friend of my parents' had worked for a moving firm, so they had all the items shipped directly to us. It was amazing! I had the opportunity to speak to everyone who came to my shower, and I laughed and cried all at the same time. I wished that I was home for this happy celebration. Homesickness began to set in. Maybe it wouldn't have been so if Terry was able to be with me at night, but having him away and being pregnant for the first time was difficult.

Nanny sensed from the conversation on the phone how scared I was, and she did the most unselfish thing anyone could do. She flew out to California to stay with me until our baby was born. Oh my God! I will never forget that feeling that I had inside when I heard that she was coming to stay with me. The shower presents were terrific, the fact that everyone came to my shower was unbelievable, but the fact that my Nanny was coming to be with me was priceless! I was in heaven, and I could never begin to thank her for this unselfish act. Things were going to be better now; I knew it.

Everyone in the complex loved Nanny, both men and women alike, but especially the women, the pregnant women. They all felt like they had their grandmother right there with them to answer questions and give advice when needed or simply to get an extra hug and kiss at a time most needed. She was our angel. Nanny played volleyball with us, took walks with us, played games and cards, and even watched the soaps on TV with us. *General Hospital* was all the rage back then. We all sat around and watched this show while eating a piece of Nanny's homemade cake or pie. Life was grand with Nanny around!

When Nanny and I took our walks along Pacific Coast Highway, the truckers would honk their horns, and we would wave and laugh. What a sight I must have been, nearly nine months pregnant and having horns blaring at me. We stopped at Taco Bell, grabbed a few tacos and a drink, and continued on with our daily walk. Of course, we had to make sure we were home in time to watch *General Hospital*.

During one episode of *General Hospital*, I started to experience severe cramping and back pain, and so Nanny asked one of my pregnant friends in the complex to drive us to the hospital as she wasn't taking any chances. We left for the hospital, and Terry was notified on board the ship that I was in labor. Thankfully, Terry's ship was still in dock, so he was able to leave the ship to be by my side for the birth of our daughter.

After many long hours of labor, our daughter was born, and we both were doing well. Many tears flowed that day, tears of happiness. As we looked at our daughter, we couldn't believe that this beautiful little girl was ours. Phone calls began flooding my hospital room with congratulations; flowers arrived, and flashes were going off, capturing every minute of our new daughter's life. We were in awe of her. We studied her and were so thankful that she was perfect... ten fingers, ten toes. I know that I studied her more carefully than usual because when I was pregnant, a horse's hoof crashed through the windshield of our car and landed right between Terry and me, so of course I screamed. I was told by some that an old wives' tale said that the baby would bear a mark from this experience, and so I was determined to check every inch of her to make sure it didn't happen. Happily, I can report this didn't happen, and she was born perfect, without a blemish.

When we came back to the apartment, Nanny continued to stay with me for some time while Terry commuted back and forth after his duties from San Diego to Long Beach. I was blessed to have Nanny with me to guide me through parenting as to what was considered normal and what was cause for concern, mainly because this was our first child. My apartment friends followed suit with their happy moments of giving birth to their first child, and Nanny was there for each one. Nanny held a very special place in each of their hearts.

The time had come when Nanny left to go back home, and I was heartbroken. I wished she could stay with me longer, but she had her responsibilities at home, and so she left. We cried, not just Terry and I but all the lovely ladies in the complex as well. Nanny cried the most, I think, having to leave her first great-grandchild. Terry had a full year left before we could head home, so this was going to be difficult being on my own once again.

My parents wrote and called, as did Nanny. After Nanny left, a feeling of being homesick came over me once again, and I just wanted to be home. I was depressed, and all I wanted was to go home for a visit with my family. I think it was a mixture of many things; just giving birth, being alone, and missing Nanny too. Terry saw it, and he knew that I needed to be home if just for a brief time, and so when my father called to say that he would pay to fly us home for a week and surprise my mother, Terry agreed. Unfortunately, Terry couldn't get any time off, so it was just the baby and I flying home. My parents hadn't seen our daughter yet or held her, so for them, this was wonderful news. My dad managed to keep a secret, and we surprised my mother. My parents were so appreciative of Terry's unselfish act, and they never forgot it.

My dad picked us up at the airport, and I hid in the back seat as he pulled into the driveway. My mother and Nanny were sitting out back at the picnic table when he pulled up. He called my mother over to the car to help him with packages, and it was then that she saw the baby and me. Oh, how she cried, and Nanny jumped right up and cried and hugged us both. I can remember that day as clearly as the day it happened. I will forever be grateful to my husband for his unselfish act by allowing us to go. It was so warming to see the look of love on everyone's faces and to witness the joy in their hearts.

Of course, my mother invited everyone over to see us, and we celebrated from the moment of our arrival. The departure was agony for all of us. Fortunately, my brother was getting married in January, so I would be flying home again to celebrate their happy day. You come to realize just how special being a part of a family is when you are without them. Never take your family for granted as they are irreplaceable. The love of family is the strongest love of all.

Upon returning to California, Terry and I moved from Long Beach to San Diego as the commute was beginning to take a toll on him, and I think he realized just how much I needed him to be with me. Several other sailors and their families moved as well, but we were never able to find a complex where we all could be together, which was truly sad. The new apartment in San Diego was nothing like what we had in Long Beach. There were no servicepeople in the development, which made us feel isolated. Thankfully, the stay there would be short as Terry soon would be finished with his tour and able to head back home. I don't think I am cut out to be far from my family and friends as I was homesick more than I care to discuss. Once Terry joined me, I felt much better, but to be home was uppermost in my mind. I enjoy traveling but not for any prolonged period. I learned that my happy place was being home.

To this day, those lovely sailors' wives and I continue to write and communicate with one another, catching up on each other's lives. Those friendships were the most memorable and special moments of being a serviceman's wife. I often reflect on these people with fond memories.

During our service years, Terry and I became soul mates. You may say that is what every lover feels, but as my story continues, you will soon realize that we were genuinely soul mates. We were a perfect fit, and to think it all began as a blind date.

Chapter 11

BACK HOME

There's nothing half as pleasant
as coming home again.
—Margaret Elizabeth Sangster

With the service years behind us, my husband and I entered a new phase in our lives. He became a law officer, and I became a teacher. Studying every minute to pass the police test was all-consuming for him. He wanted this career more than anything, and he worked diligently to achieve his goal. I was so proud of him when he was called to join the men in blue. His mother, my parents, Nanny, and of course I myself were thrilled that his dreams were now going to become a reality. He had found a career that had a purpose, and he was proud of his accomplishments.

Now that Terry was a police officer and I was a teacher, it afforded us the opportunity to move out of our apartment and purchase a home. It was the American dream to be a homeowner, and that dream was ours. Our first home was a row home on a tree-lined street. We had a lovely patio where many happy times were shared with neighbors, families, and friends. There were many young couples just starting out like us on our street, which made it that much more enticing.

Terry worked tirelessly on converting the basement into a nice recreation room He was very handy with his hands, knowing how to build, wallpaper, lay tiles, paint, and design a specific look. This project took a large sum of money to convert the basement into a recreation room, especially since we both had expensive taste. Many times, we didn't have the pocketbook or bank account to have such expensive taste, but in the end, the final project was beautiful and well worth the sacrifice. We were living the American dream.

Shortly after, I found out that I was expecting our second child. Our first daughter was now almost four years old when her baby sister would make her grand entrance.

Our lives were headed in the right direction, or so I thought. We had a beautiful family, home, and successful careers. I noticed changes in my husband, and try as I might, I couldn't get him to open up and talk to me about what was wrong. My mind started to think of all the worse scenarios, such as was he ill, did he lose his job, were we deeper in debt than I thought, was he unhappy with me, or worse yet, did he find someone new to replace me?

I was sick thinking about what it could be, and being who I am, I needed to know. How could I fix something if I didn't have a clue what it was that was bothering him? There is nothing worse than beating your head against the wall trying to get answers from your spouse when they completely shut you out. I know that I became a nag, searching for what was wrong and receiving the same answer repeatedly that it was nothing. He made me feel like I was going crazy, telling me that there was nothing wrong and that I was imagining these things. He made me question myself, and at times, I did feel like I was cracking up, but I knew for certain that he was not the same man that I married; he was the one who changed. Not only did his silence give away that something was wrong, but his body language did as well. I felt like he was avoiding me every chance that he could. I felt even though he was home with me, he was someplace else, and this treatment was killing me. If only he would open up and speak to me about whatever it was, maybe then I could help him. Perhaps I was feeling like this because I was pregnant. Only time would tell.

I tried putting this feeling to rest, but it continued to gnaw at me. My gut kept saying there was so much more to this than I knew, and so I decided to venture out to find some answers since my husband wasn't giving me any. As I began eliminating one possibility after another, I was left only with the option that he was cheating. When that realization struck me, I recall sitting on the stairs of our home and crying a heart-wrenching cry that was similar to the day when my Nanny, mother, and father passed away.

I felt my life slipping away from me. I couldn't bring myself to believe that the man I loved so deeply was cheating on me and found comfort in another woman's arms. The more I thought about it, the sicker I became. How could this be true? How could the man I love hurt me like this? What did I do that was that terrible for him to cheat, and why couldn't we have talked it over? Why couldn't we have gone to a marriage counselor to resolve this? I just kept asking myself these questions as I continued to sob. Why? How could this happen?

Things started to change in our marriage after Terry became a policeman. Shift work interfered with our family life, and I felt that too often, I was doing things alone with the children. His shift work caused him to sleep when we were awake, and trying to keep small children quiet during the day was difficult, especially since they were little and tended to be noisy. I knew he needed his rest so that he could go to work, and many times, I would leave the house with the girls so that the house was quiet for him. We'd go to the park, take a walk, or go over to my parent's home. We'd see Terry before he left for work and then we'd be alone again. I'd get the girls ready for bed and then retire myself.

It was like we were ships passing in the night. I worked in the day, and he worked different shifts. I was tired and ready for bed, and he'd be wide awake. I believe this created a problem, which was causing us to lose each other. We rarely had quality time with each other. Day work was better because we were able to have meals together, talk, and share fun times with the children or with each other.

I was consumed with my obligations as a teacher, planning and creating crafty ideas to get the children interested in the lessons. I was given more responsibilities at school, which required more of my time and energy. I think all of these factored into our marital problems too. It wasn't just him, which I came to realize and accept as time went on. Being swamped with being both a mother and a career woman, compounded with his crazy shifts and overtime, we were left with very little time together, which was a significant problem in our relationship.

Chapter 12

CHANGES

Trust is like paper—once it's crumpled,
it can't be perfect again.
—Mashavils

My feelings that cheating was the cause for the changes in my husband continued to fester, and his denial that anything was wrong or there was another woman in the picture didn't lessen my fears. My gut instinct told me he was lying, and the reason for his silence more than likely was because he was afraid to tell me the truth, knowing how I'd react. I think it was easier for him to lie than to be truthful. I had no concrete proof, but this feeling continued to gnaw at me day in and day out.

Soon, there were phone calls when he was home, and whenever I answered, the other party hung up. At first, I thought it was a wrong number, but then these calls and hang-ups became more frequent. The hang-ups only occurred when I answered the phone, and they were occurring more frequently, like his days off or shortly before he was heading out the door to report to work. If I didn't beat him to the phone (where the other party would hang up) and he got to the phone, he would lower his voice and then come up with a story that it was work, which I sensed was a lie. This led to me questioning him and his denying it. He told me that I was paranoid, but I knew differently.

This woman was relentless with her calling. She was bold and would stop at nothing just to get him to talk to her on the phone. My mind wandered into thoughts like, who was she, where did she live, where did he meet her, how often did they meet up, was he sleeping with her? It was torture living like this, knowing that he was lying and trying to figure out what I did that was so wrong that made him want to move on. I couldn't wrap my mind around how he was able to hurt me like this. I wouldn't do this to him. When he came home, I would look at him and wonder if he spent time with her before coming back to me. It put a wedge between us and made me more suspicious each day. When I did the wash, I'd check his pockets to see if there was anything in them, like a note or phone number, and smell his shirts to see if there was a scent of perfume that wasn't mine.

No one should live this way. It consumed me with feelings that I never experienced before; outrage, bitterness, hate, wanting revenge, and a sense of feeling powerless. I know I tried to get to the truth, but did I honestly want to hear it? I kept hoping that my gut was wrong, jumping to conclusions without any real evidence, but I could not shake this horrible feeling. Months and months went on with these feelings, being tormented and betrayed, and wondering every time that he came home late or said he was working overtime, was he really? I am sure being pregnant didn't help as I was more emotional, and I needed him and his love more now than ever.

Trust was a major issue for me after all these months of strange behaviors and feelings that I was being lied to over and over again. I questioned him so much and argued with him over these suspicions, and his answer was always the same. He wasn't seeing anyone. Lie after lie, he told me, and I knew it deep down in my gut.

When our youngest daughter was born and I was in the hospital waiting to deliver her, my mother called the district, as my husband was working the night shift, and asked them to notify Terry that I was in labor and to please head to the hospital. My father drove me while my mother was at home with our oldest daughter, who was sleeping. The police department got in touch with my husband, who came to the hospital, but by that time, I was already in the delivery room.

Back then, husbands were not permitted in the delivery room as they are today, so I had no idea if he was there waiting for the news or not. All I remember was being wheeled into the delivery room, gazing into my father's eyes, who promised me that everything would be okay and that he loved me. These were the last words that I remembered as I was heading to the delivery room. I needed and wanted to hear these words from my husband. Where was he? Why wasn't he here? With that I dozed off.

When I was taken to my room after giving birth to our cute bundle of joy, our second daughter, Terry was waiting for me with flowers and stayed at my bedside. He told me how beautiful our little girl was and how proud he was of me. I remember looking into his eyes and thinking how lucky we were to have two beautiful and healthy girls. Our baby girl was precious. She was perfect and had such an adorable smile. We truly were blessed. He stayed with me for a while and then headed home to be with our oldest daughter.

The following morning, my room was adorned with roses, plants, balloons, and adorable girly outfits for the baby. I received many phone calls, congratulating us on our new baby girl. It was a joyous moment, that was *until* I received a phone call from a woman I never met. Her voice was cold and evil as were her words. She said, "Your husband was with me last night while you were giving birth. We both wish that she was ours." I couldn't believe what I was hearing. She went on to tell me that she had been with my husband for a while now and that they would be together. It was the cruelest thing anyone could have ever done to another person, let alone a woman who had just given birth.

I loathe this woman from the deepest depths of my soul. I thought there was a moral code between women, and you don't come between a husband and a wife and their family, but I guess this woman never was taught this. She was evil through and through and so heartless. My anger and hurt elevated to the point that I had no words for her; I was speechless, and I hung up the phone—more like I slammed the phone down—and then cried uncontrollably.

When the nurse came in to check on the baby and me, she noticed that I was crying. Maybe at first, she thought I had postpartum depression, until I asked her to stay with me for a minute, which she did. In between my sobbing, I recounted the phone call that I had just received from the other woman. The nurse couldn't believe the cruelty of this woman, and she tried her best to console me.

There were no words of comfort; my worst fears came true with that evil and heartless phone call. How could anyone be so cruel? This was to be a joyous moment, and she had to be so evil as to make this call. I put two and two together and realized this was the person who was calling and hanging up on me, the one who was destroying our marriage. Now, I needed to find out just who she was.

Terry brought the baby and me home, and family and friends stopped by to see us. He was very loving and devoted as he cared for us, but I knew in the pit of my stomach that this would probably be short-lived. I didn't tell him about that phone call that I received from that harlot that day because I didn't want to let him know that I knew. I felt confident that she would never tell him herself and risk him being angry at her, so I knew this conversation was safe until I wanted to reveal it. I wanted to find this evil harlot first, and then he would know about her evil, vile act that caused me so much pain after the birth of our precious daughter.

Months went on, and Terry continued to be caring and attentive to his family, but I lost trust in him, and once you lose that trust, it is difficult to get it back, especially when the phone calls continued to pour into our home. I was now on a mission to find her and see if she meant anything to him, or was she merely a fling, a mistake? This home-wrecker had one thing on her mind, I am sure of that, and that was to be with a cop.

She never left him alone as I found out one day when I went to open the trunk to place items in it and saw gift boxes with articles of clothing still in their boxes along with her love notes. Why did he leave them in the trunk of the car, knowing that I would have to open it to put the baby things inside? Was he hoping that I would find these items and the secret would be out? Every time I asked about this woman, I had the same response from him—nothing was going on. Little did he know that I had evidence that something was going on and that I was determined to find her! Whoever would be so bold as to call the wife of the man you are seeing on the day she gave birth and say that she was with your husband was a monster!

She could care less about breaking up our family because she was intent on getting what she wanted. I read about women like her, saw them in movies, but never in my life did I think I would have to encounter one of these selfish, heartless women. I hadn't met her, but I certainly knew I hated her.

I called my best friend and confided in her what my suspicions were and asked her to watch my girls after I bathed them and put them to bed so that I could drive down to the district and wait outside to see for myself who this home-wrecker was. Her first response was that she didn't believe he was involved with anyone. She tried to tell me that maybe it was the woman who was pursuing my husband, and he was trying to steer clear of her, and that she was the one who was determined to see him and was manipulating him. I believed that at one point too, but if that were the case, he could have told me, and we could have worked through this together, but he kept it a secret.

I restated to her again how crucial it was for me to check it out, and I needed her to stay with the girls for a little while, to which she finally agreed. I prayed all the way down there that I was wrong and that he would leave the station alone, but that wasn't the case, and my worst fears were confirmed. As he came down the steps of the station, she was walking up to greet him. They kissed, and my heart sunk. I quickly drew the courage to get out of the car, and I approached him. Terry was horrified to see me, I am sure, and she was as bold as could be hanging on to his arm.

The look on his face is one that I will never forget. He looked sad, and to this day, I'm not sure if he was sorry that I caught him or sad that he hurt me. Either way, there she was, so brazen and so bold, standing on the steps. I wanted to beat her to a bloody pulp, but I wouldn't stoop to her level, nor would I embarrass my husband at his place of work.

I gathered up a little more courage and asked him if he was coming home with me or not? Basically, I was asking, "Who do you choose? Who are you coming home with?" He didn't answer quickly enough for me, and I knew then and there that it was over. I wanted him to answer me right away, in a flash, without hesitation, that he was coming home with his family and me, but that slight hesitation/ pause was all I needed. I felt that was his answer, and I was not going to plead for any man's love. I refuse to settle for not being his only love. I really should have known my husband better and not overreacted because he never answered a question quickly. He always ponders on his answers, taking his time, so this incident was no different. I should have given him the wait time and just waited to see what his response would have been, but at that moment, I thought it was a sign, and I took it to mean he didn't care.

I was heartbroken, sick to my stomach, and wept all the way home. My girlfriend couldn't believe it. She tried to convince me that he probably was in shock to see me there and didn't know what to say, but I didn't see it that way at all. I cried for days, and no matter how he tried to explain what had happened, I wasn't listening. I was tired of the lies, and to be quite honest, what reasoning could he give me for having another woman meeting him after work at his workplace and kissing him?

Sorry, but there was no excuse for this—absolutely none! All that ran through my mind as I thought about what I witnessed was we used to be soul mates and so close. I gave my heart to this man. How did this happen? What went wrong? I felt so violated. I was not accustomed to being treated like this. I had a father who loved me and made sacrifices for me to assure my happiness and well-being. I thought this man was like my father, based on how he used to treat me. Where did I go wrong? What a fool I was ever to believe that love was forever like my parents'.

To make matters worse, even after I confronted him with her at his side, she boldly continued to call the house and hang up when I answered. She was a gold digger, a home-wrecker, and I could tell that she had her claws into my husband, and she had no intentions of letting him go.

To this day, I cannot come to grips with how a woman could so easily hurt another. She was just plain evil! She had a lack of respect for the sanctity of marriage and family. She could have chosen to walk away, not get involved with a married man, as could he, but she had so much more to gain than he did. She wanted a daddy for her two girls, security that his job would offer, and the financial means to go places and do things that only he could give. She wasn't a professional woman, nor was she highly educated, so hooking up with my husband would give her the prestige and security she lacked on her own.

As for him, sex was something he could have whenever he desired with her, I guess, and he wasn't thinking about the consequences. She was a manipulator, a user, and poison like a snake that strikes and goes after what she wants, stopping at nothing until she gets it. It was evident that she didn't care about ruining our relationship or our family; all she cared about was her own happiness. She robbed my family's right to happiness, to be a family, and hopefully, she will reap the rewards someday for her evil doings. Karma has a way of catching up with people who do evil things!

I questioned myself over and over again as to what caused this. Did I spend too much time caring for the children? Did I put my career before my husband? Could I have spent less time on work and more time with my husband? The tormenting questions went on, and with each question, I felt that cheating still was not the solution. We continued to live in the same house for some time and tried to work things out, but it never was the same. The trust was gone, and every time he came home a few minutes late, I wondered, *If he was with her?* I didn't want to see what once was love turn into hate, and I knew that we needed to part. This one act broke my heart and our future. Not only did the cheating affect the girls and me, but many other people suffered from this as well.

This repugnant woman was street-smart. She was a fighter. She reminded me of a black widow, going after what she wanted and then capturing it. She did just that! Maybe if there was some fight left in me, I would have fought harder, but trust continually crept up, and I hated not being able to trust him. As much as I loved him, I was not going to be second best for anyone. I loved him and would never have thought he was capable of cheating. I am a fighter, but as soon as the trust left our relationship, a switch went off in my head, and I could think of nothing else but her ruining our life. I knew that he would see her every day as she was a waitress in the area, and I couldn't be sure that he would stay away or that she wouldn't attempt to see him every day or night after work. She was bold and not trustworthy. He said he wanted to work things out, but I no longer could trust him.

As time went on, I came to find out that she had two daughters from two different men, and she was a single parent. I'm sure she wanted a better life for herself and her girls, and what better way than to get hooked up with a police officer? She knew what she was doing. She played her cards right. She played the helpless, needy mother who would leave her girls to pursue a relationship with a man who could make her life better.

How could she go out on these dates with him and leave her young girls home alone to care for themselves? Well, she did, and that certainly didn't bother her. She was only interested in her own pleasure, leaving her children unattended night after night.

When I found out that her two girls were close in age to our two girls that hurt even more. How could he be with her and her two kids when he had daughters of his own at home? It was mind-boggling to me. Our girls were being denied their father so that hers could have one, yet she denied her second daughter the right to know who her real father was. She was so conniving and calculating that when her second daughter was born, she lied to her, gave her the first daughter's last name when that man wasn't even her father. The real father tried to get in touch with his daughter, but this woman never allowed that to occur. Evil through and through, and now she was taking away my two daughters' father to play daddy with hers. If this isn't the definition of evil, then I don't know what is.

I couldn't understand how my husband couldn't see this for what it was. He is a smart man. If it were a friend of his going through this, I know what his advice would be to that friend, and yet he strayed and believed her lies, leaving the children without their father and me without my husband. Maybe if I didn't care that he had a fling on the side, it would have worked, but that is not in my makeup, and I'm sure that home-wrecker—or as the Bible would say, harlot— would never step back and move on to a new victim. She had her claws out, and she wanted him totally for herself.

As hard as I wanted to save this marriage, I couldn't believe or forgive Terry when he said he was sorry. He could have stopped his visits with her, made her stop calling the house and torturing me, and even put in for a transfer, but he didn't. He was a police officer, and I know something could have been done if he really wanted to end this. My parents tried numerous times to convince me to take time and let this run its course, to get counseling and work on saving our marriage. They tried reasoning with me and told me to think about the consequences that would be by ending our marriage, but the hurt was just too deep, and there was one thing that I knew: I would not or could not be second best to anyone.

What kept running through my head was what if we had an argument, would he run right to her? He saw her every day when he went to work, so how could I be sure that when he said it was over that it was? I could no longer live worrying each day if he were mine or not? Every time the phone rang, would it be her again? It's no way to live, and if the shoe was on the other foot and it was me who was having an affair, would my husband be okay with that? Would he not question my coming home later than I said, or the strange hang-ups that frequented our home? Would he understand? Would he suffer pain as I did when these things occurred? I am sure he would be just as distraught as I was. So for me, I had to take a stand, and so I set him free. Like the saying goes, "If you love someone, set them free. If it is meant to be, they will return to you."

I felt strongly that this woman, who played a crucial role in breaking up our marriage and our family, would never let us work on repairing our marriage. Like I alluded to before, she was a gold digger who was looking out for herself and her daughters, regardless of the pain that it cost our daughters or us. I realize that both Terry and I had our issues, our faults, but with counseling, I felt we could have gotten past these issues and worked toward rebuilding what some-how got lost along the way. As long as this viper was in the picture, it would never work. Even if he asked to be transferred to another district, she would have hounded him. She set her mind on having him, and she was determined that's how it would be. No one does the things that she did (called the day our baby was born to tell me she was having an affair, lie to her own child about her birthright) just to walk away because he wanted his family and not her. She was relentless in pursuing him, a woman without a conscience.

When we tried to work things out, she always surfaced her disgusting face, and there was just no stopping her. It was as though she sensed when we were trying to get back together, and she immediately interfered. She would be the fatal attraction. She knew that Terry was a good man and that he would not report her for continually harassing me, so she was empowered to do her dirty tricks with no consequences.

It was me that pursued the divorce, as difficult as it was, and I had Terry served with the divorce papers. I knew it was time to let go. I was exhausted, physically and emotionally drained, and this situation was suffocating me. I was filled with such hatred for her, and I couldn't allow hatred to define me. I felt I would be better being alone, having my self-respect again—my dignity—than to remain in a situation that I had unfortunately found myself in. I no longer could bear the pain, torment, or humiliation, and so I emptied our house of the things that belonged to the children and me, and we left. I didn't care about the house; he could sell it or live in it because all that it held for me now were unhappy memories.

Terry and I had previously purchased tickets to take our oldest daughter to a concert, and I was now planning on going by myself with our daughter. Terry left me a note on the dining room table, asking if he could please join us as planned. Since the concert was a gift for our daughter, I thought it was only right to ask her if she wanted her daddy to come, and she did. After asking to join us at the concert, he continued to express his feelings in writing. He was better at putting his feelings down on paper than speaking, especially after all that we had been through lately. The note read,

> "Before I go I would just like to say how deeply sorry I am for the misery and grief that I've caused you. I wrecked our lives in fine fashion. I've thrown away a love I know that I couldn't find again in a million years. I am sure that God

will justly reward my actions. As I am sure that I
will regret them for the rest of my life. I hope that
someday you will forgive me, it's a lot to ask, but
I'm hoping anyway."

I cried as I read this letter, and if she were out of the picture, I
know that we could have made it, but those nasty calls and hang-ups
continued to go on and on, and I doubted his love for us whenever
he wasn't home. Maybe he really wanted to try again, but his mis-
tress was having no part of it, and so with heavy hearts, we went our
separate ways.

Terry left behind a book for me entitled *Our Inward Journey*
with a handwritten letter about his feelings and how this book clearly
laid out his thoughts. The book "explores the quiet world that lies
within us all." It was beautifully written and expressed both of us
perfectly. He wrote, "Through all my life you have been my dearest,
closest and only true friend. You have also been the one I have the
hardest time expressing myself to, and that shouldn't be." He further
went on, saying, "My outwardly attitude is a disguise to camouflage
the fact that I am and have been for a long time, mad and disgusted
with myself for past and present failures…bad decisions, the wrong
choices." I kept this book as well as his letters and read and reread
these words throughout the years.

I moved into an apartment with the children. So many times I
felt powerless, but I knew that I couldn't give up, or it would be over.
I had to stand up for my children and myself and remain strong. I
was about to travel down a different path, and if ever I needed to be
strong, it was now. When the final divorce papers were delivered, I
cried for hours as this really wasn't something that I wanted. Terry
recalls crying as well, in disbelief that our lives were over. The sick
feeling in the pit of my stomach was unending. I wished this was
all a bad dream, a nightmare, and that when I woke up, it was over.
Reality set in quickly, and I knew that my life as I knew it was now
a thing of the past. Neither one of us wanted the divorce, which was
a tragedy, but this other woman who entered our lives changed that
forever. And so, our new lives began, sadly, without each other.

Chapter 13

ON MY OWN

Being strong doesn't mean you'll never
get hurt. It means that when you do get
hurt, you'll never let it defeat you.

The pain of divorce is unbearable. I now had to face the realization that I was a single mother of two little girls who needed me and that there was no time to think about how I was hurting or what I was feeling. My life and attention needed to be on the children. My parents helped by watching the girls when I worked, so I knew they were loved and well cared for. My parents helped me find an apartment and get my new life on track.

Being a single mother of two was a full-time job. I found that I had very little time to think about what I lost because I was so absorbed with taking on the role of mother and father as well as provider. That is not to say that their father didn't provide for his children because he did, but it was worrying about all the extra little things that children need to keep their lives as normal as possible. Softball, skating lessons, bowling events, friends' birthday parties, sleepovers soon began to take up a lot of my free time.

Weekends with their dad began to dwindle, and I don't know who bears the blame for that. Was it his decision, hers, or did the children just shift gears and decide being home with their friends was more fun? Whatever the reason, time soon put a distance between them. Selfishly, I was relieved that he stopped coming around because every time that I saw him, I thought about what we once had and how much I still loved him. Seeing her in the passenger seat infuriated me, and I wanted to walk up to the car and inflict pain on her as she did me, but in the end, what would that have accomplished? I chose to end this marriage, but I wished over and over again that I had listened to my parents' advice and tried to make it work. That is a lesson and a regret that I had to learn on my own and then live with. When I saw him, I wondered each time he saw me, did he feel the same things that I was feeling?

She could have encouraged the father-daughter relationship, but she didn't. I felt then, and still do now, that she helped to create the parent alienation by not trying to keep a relationship going between Terry and his children. She created that wedge between families, causing our girls to feel uncomfortable around her. They were treated differently whenever they were in her company, and she always needed to be present when they visited. The girls said they felt weird at their house because they never could spend time talking to their dad alone. They were hurt when her daughters would call Terry "dad" or when they would be out and her daughters introduced Terry as "their dad" while they were standing right next to him. I asked why they never spoke up, and their comment was, "For what purpose?" They learned to live with it and gradually saw him less and less.

To this day, I still believe it was all about her and her two girls. Her interest was to better her life and that of her kids, which left mine out. Should he have worked harder to see his biological daughters? Absolutely! Did he love his girls? I strongly believe he did. Did he support his daughters and provide for them? Absolutely, *but* rather than argue with her, he chose to do as she directed and, therefore, regretfully missed out on so much of his daughters' lives.

I often thought that she was worried if he came here for the girls and we spoke and saw each other, that the flame we felt when we first met might just rekindle. You know what they say, when you do underhanded things to others, it might just backfire, and I think she was worried about that happening. I believe she wanted her girls to become the substitute for his girls and for him to be involved in their lives, which he was.

Her two girls attended private school for a while because she could now afford it with his income, while our daughters were fortunate enough to attend also, but that was thanks to the support of my family and sister-in-law. Had it not been for their financial support, the girls would not have been so fortunate. She had a scheme, an evil plan, and it was our children who paid the price. The more I got to know this woman, the more I realized just what a spiteful and pathetic excuse for a woman, a human being, she was.

I sent him a birthday card every year as well as a Christmas card and later found out that he never knew that I sent him a birthday card. I guess the cards were taken out of the mailbox before he ever saw them. Maybe she wasn't so sure that it was really over between the two of us, and that is why she removed them from the mailbox. If it wasn't her, then it was her girls because I sent them every year, and they were never returned to me.

After our divorce, I had heard that Terry was involved in a motorcycle accident while on duty. Someone cut him out, and he flew over the windshield and landed in the middle of the highway. He tore most muscles from his waist down and was out of work for close to a month. After our daughters informed me of this accident, I went to his apartment to visit him and to see if he needed anything. I had to see firsthand that he was on the mend as he had been badly banged up, and I felt sorry for him and thankful that God spared his life. Looking in his eyes, I felt his pain, and I thought what I saw was not only physical pain but emotional pain as well. I sensed that both of us were wishing that the outcome of our marriage was different. The words were unspoken, but our eyes said it all. He thanked me for coming, and I left.

Seeing him again, looking in his eyes, stirred up many different emotions. It is such a sad thing to still be so much in love with someone and know that they aren't yours anymore. Did he think about what we had and miss it as I did? Did a song on the radio bring back special memories of tender moments together? I knew seeing him face to face that I was still in love with him, and it hurt each time. There is an emptiness that no one can fill. All I could do now was to pray for his safety each night and hope that he was happy. I hope that there are times that he thinks about me, as I do him, and what could have been.

When he returned to work a month later, he was assigned to an unmarked cruiser for six months and then reassigned to the motorcycle, which he loved.

Through the years, I saw him a few times at the mall or at a store. I always chose to walk down another aisle so as not to be noticed and looked at him from afar, thinking and wishing that I had another chance to love this man and be loved again by him. After our breakup, walking through the mall, seeing couples holding hands, laughing, stealing a quick kiss as they strolled from store to store was painful; these were some of the fondest memories we shared. I wondered if he ever had flashbacks to our times together as I did. I passed by a restaurant that we ate in, a park that we picnicked in, or even the bowling alley where we spent endless hours, as he bowled in tournaments, and wondered, *Did any of these places cause him to reflect on happier times together?* Even the movie theater where we hung out in our younger days, our first home, the church where we were married were all part of my cherished memories, and I wondered, *Were they his too?* Funny how it never mattered where we went just as long as we were together.

I was in his company on a few occasions, such as the girls' graduation, his mother's funeral, and our younger daughter's wedding. We'd hug and give each other a kiss on the cheek, and for that moment, it felt right. There were moments when his hug and kiss let me believe these thoughts were his as well. With each encounter, I stared at him, wishing I was standing beside him and not her. I thought many times about contacting him and telling him what a mistake I had made by not trying harder to work through our problems instead of running away from them, but then I remembered that horrible feeling that I had the day that I learned he found someone else, and I didn't want to ever experience that pain again. I guess I didn't call him or try to get in touch with him because I was afraid of what his response would have been.

There were times that I honestly felt I had the right to make a move and see what would happen because my feelings weren't considered years ago, but I didn't, and so I lived without the one man that made me the happiest. If you would ask me today if I would do things differently, you bet I would. First, I wouldn't have gotten a divorce, and I most certainly would have put her in her place. She would have seen a side of me that she would never want to mess with. She never once considered my feelings or my children's, so yes, today I would not think twice about going after the man I loved. But that didn't happen, and so my life as well as his changed forever.

I always remember what my mother said to me when I told her how I wished we were still together. She repeated a saying that I said over and over in my head, which was, "If you love something set it free. If it comes back to you, then it was meant to be." God, how I wished this would be the case for us.

With the passing of time, I met another man who was kind to my girls and treated me well. It was no longer about me and my feelings but who was good to my children. I didn't go out and date as my time was with my children, who needed more of my love and time, not less, since I divorced their father. My meeting with the man who would later become my second husband came about by chance, I guess you could say. While working at the bank, he was a steady customer, and one thing led to another. He had asked me out for dinner, I accepted, and it continued from there. I kept my children out of this relationship as I didn't want anyone hurting them until I was sure that this was the right relationship and they were safe. They had gone through enough in their young lives, and I would not want to see them hurt again. When I finally agreed they could meet him and felt that it was safe, I made sure that we did family things every weekend. Our weekends were with the girls, unless they were with their father.

Knowing that I would never get a second chance with my first husband, I eventually married for the second time. The feelings and emotions felt were undoubtedly different with him than with my first husband. My heart didn't skip a beat every time I saw him; it didn't feel the same at all. No one was ever going to take the place of my first husband. This man was a good man, but things just felt different.

Chapter 14

A NEW RELATIONSHIP

It is hard to tell your mind to stop loving
someone if your heart still does.

"You might get attracted to another person
but you won't simply fall in love if someone
else is still holding a BIG part of your heart."
—Unknown

I guess being a single mother with two young girls, knowing I had
to make it on my own, scared me, so I rushed into a relationship
without giving it the proper time that I should have to weigh all the
pros and cons of being married again. I was now responsible for three
lives, and I needed to help my girls live a happy, normal life without
their dad. Looking back, I realize how foolish I was because *I am* a
strong woman, and *I could* have made it on my own. My girls would
have still had the things they needed as children because their father
would have helped give them these things as would my parents and
his family if I had asked.

I wanted to be loved by a man so badly, to feel valued and special that I guess when this man came along and gave me all things
that I was missing, I jumped into a relationship. I should have taken
more time being on my own because had I done so, I never would
have remarried. My parents and Nanny were not happy, nor were my
closest friends, because they knew my true feelings, which was that I
was still in love with my first husband. In hindsight, I married for all

the wrong reasons, and I wasn't being true to myself or to my second husband.

In the beginning, life was good. We were happy, and it felt good to be needed and loved. The girls seemed happy, and we did many things together as a family. It was such a peaceful feeling to be a complete family once again. Over the course of this marriage, we were blessed with two more beautiful girls. I struggled to get pregnant with our daughter and had to seek professional help, test after test, to determine if I could have another child. I had no difficulty getting pregnant with my first and second daughter, so why was this any different? Maybe it was due to my age; I really didn't know.

In time, my third daughter arrived, and I felt blessed. In between her birth and the birth of her sister, I hemorrhaged while taking a shower. I was standing in a pool of my own blood and called for my oldest daughter, who was in the living room. She grabbed towels and wanted to call the ambulance, but I said no. I asked her to watch her two sisters so that I could drive to the hospital. She did, and I drove myself with towels to control the bleeding between my legs. I don't know how I made it there, but I did.

Upon arrival to the emergency room, I stumbled in, blood running down my legs onto the floor, as white as a ghost. I walked to the desk and told the nurse that I was hemorrhaging and that I thought I was going to faint. She immediately came over to me with a wheelchair and that was all that I remembered until I woke up in a bed. I had an emergency DNC, and I lost a lot of blood. They suggested a transfusion, but I didn't want one. My father immediately arrived at the hospital and offered his blood since I was adamant about not receiving a transfusion, but they said I should be fine and to wait and see.

My girls came to visit as well. I felt so sorry for the older two as they were scared, and I can only imagine what a scary sight that must have been to witness. There was another visitor who came to check on me to see that I was okay and to see if I needed anything: my first husband. I couldn't believe that he came. The girls told their dad that I was in the hospital, and without hesitation, he stopped to check on me and to see that I was okay. It was obvious that we both still cared for one another even though we were living separate lives. I honestly can say that I don't remember my second husband coming to see me, but in fairness, he was an over-the-road driver and quite possibly he could not get there.

Shortly after this incident, I became pregnant with my last child—my fourth daughter. It was a miracle that I had her because I really wasn't supposed to be able to have any more children. My second husband was not at all sensitive to this pregnancy. He didn't offer to help me during this time. He continually worried about himself and his needs. It was really unbelievable. I was carrying his child, and all he could do was worry about himself. If it wasn't for the two older girls helping me with their sisters and around the house, I would have had zero help through this pregnancy.

My second husband would come home from work and want to go out to grab a bite to eat with his friends. When I wasn't up to going, he became angry and would go himself. Time after time, this happened. On another incident, I was so sick and weak that I couldn't get out of bed. He came home, demanded that we go out with his friends, to which I replied, "I am sick. I am not up to it. Can't you see that?" He told me that "I could die for all he cared" and walked out for an evening with his friends. Things like this don't go unnoticed and certainly aren't forgotten. His lack of empathy and selfishness were drawing a wedge between our relationship. How does a person who is supposed to love you leave you to go out for the evening when you are pregnant and violently ill? This by no means is what I call love.

My older girls from my first marriage unfortunately had to take on more than any child should. They helped me through a very difficult time. They were so good to their baby sisters. They became very close through the years, and their love for each other is unconditional. Being a mother was the most important thing to me, and having four girls was truly a blessing. I have to honestly say that the best part of my second marriage were my two daughters. I would never have had them had I not been married again, and that would have been a terrible loss. I love these girls with all my heart, and thanks to them, they have helped make me a stronger and better person.

Like Dr. Jekyll and Mr. Hyde, my second husband would surprise us by doing thoughtful things. He surprised my oldest daughter on her Confirmation Day by making sure he'd make it to the ceremony even though he was an over-the-road driver. When we left to go to the church, he wasn't home yet, but as the ceremony went on, there he was, standing in the back of the church. It meant a lot to my daughter because he kept his promise and was there for her with a bouquet of flowers. Sadly, these moments were few and far between.

He had a daughter from a previous marriage, so we spent many of our weekends traveling to spend time with our extended families. The girls all got along, and his daughter was close in age to my second child, so the times with the children were enjoyable. Looking back, I see how spending time with the children was really the only thing in common that we had. We were total opposites, with different views on just about everything. His likes were my dislikes, and my likes were his dislikes. We were mixed matched. One time I made a compare-and-contrast sheet on us, and it was both enlightening as well as scary. We really didn't belong together.

Things were much different with this relationship. We were never soul mates, and we really didn't have much in common. I guess I thought that different was good; after all, my first husband and I had so much in common, and look what path that lead us down.

I always thought about my parents' marriage and how beautiful it was. They never argued in front of my brother or me, and they respected one another. They worked together for a common goal and talked endlessly about their plans. I think I was secretly searching for a marriage like theirs, and to be frank, I was searching for a man like my father. I thought I found that with my first husband, but my father never cheated and hurt my mother, like my husband did to me, or deserted his children. I guess there is only one person who is just like my father and that is my father.

Chapter 15

LOVE TURNED TO HATE

If there is a worse place than hell, I am in it.
—Abraham Lincoln

Things began to turn sour after some years. My second husband began showing his true colors. He was both controlling and demanding. I wasn't accustomed to yelling, not in my growing up years or in my first marriage. He would raise his voice in such a way that made me tremble inside, and from then on, fear took over.

During one of our visits to see his daughter, I learned after I married him from his first wife how terrified she was of him, how violent he could be, and I began to piece things together. She had court documents that she shared with me, along with the protection from abuse order for her and her daughter, and now I felt fear for the first time. I needed to protect myself and my children. They were my first concern, and it was evident that I had to learn more about keeping us safe. I learned how to become an actress, keeping my true feelings hidden, so as not to alert him that I really feared him. Had he known that I was becoming afraid of him, it would be all over.

Spring came, and with the change of seasons, his mood changed as well. He seemed happier and more content. He decided that he was going to make much-needed repairs on the house with his friend's help. We purchased a new shower enclosure along with sink and toilet as the bathroom was in dire need of an upgrade. In order to make these changes, the bathroom was gutted. He completely tore the bathroom apart, removed the oil burner from the kitchen area to give that a total overhaul, and the washer had to be disconnected as that was in the kitchen area as well. This was a major operation and created quite a mess as well as inconvenience.

Every night, his friend faithfully came over to work on this project with him. Weekends were absorbed in this as well. Needless to say, the house was a disaster, which often times is the case when major projects are underway, but this was ridiculous. We are talking about not having a bathroom to use on the first floor (had one on the second floor, thank God), not having a washer at my disposal (family of six), and no heat or hot water except for a hot water hookup that was created until the bathroom and heater were fixed. The oil burner in the kitchen provided us with our heat and hot water, and this was removed to be rebuilt.

Out in the backyard, the oil tank was leaning up against one of the sheds; the heater had been gutted, and it sat in the yard with the oil containers for several weeks, along with the newly purchased shower enclosure that he had insisted needed to be purchased ahead of time. It sat for close to four weeks along with all the other items that had been disassembled. Luckily, the weather was decent as it was the end of August / beginning of September when this undertaking was happening. This project was massive, and it wasn't being done on a daily basis full-time; rather, it was being done when time permitted. This project, which was supposed to be done in a week or two, tops, was now dragging into six weeks.

I was busy preparing for my granddaughter's Christening and needed his help to at least get some things back in order so that I could entertain guests at the house. The invitations were sent with the thought that the remodeling would have been completed, as promised, and now it was too late to cancel or have the party elsewhere. I was in a panic because there were many family and friends coming to the Christening, and so I asked him to please put back the washer in the kitchen and put the items that were all over the house in the back shed for the party. I knew I would have to leave well enough alone with the condition of the bathroom, and so I decided to shut the door as if it didn't exist. Surprisingly, he agreed to do as I asked without an argument, but maybe that was because his friend was here working on the bathroom with him at the time. Having a positive response put me in shock, and all I could say was, "Thank you."

Now the work begins. The house was still a mess from this project, and I had much to do. Aside from the scrubbing and cleaning, I had cooking, decorating, and setting up for this event. She was my first grandchild, and I wanted her day to be as special as she was. I had to accept what I had to work with and try my best to make the house look as nice as possible. I needed a fairy godmother! It was family and friends who were coming to the party, and they knew about this project, so the only real mess was in the first floor bathroom, which was closed; the kitchen was missing the oil burner, but I managed to cover that area with a table and placed items on it; and of course, the backyard, where there was nothing that I could really do to improve that disaster. The company could sit out front instead was my thinking if they needed to be outside.

As we were busy moving things around, he asked where my daughter was and why she wasn't helping. I said she was putting the baby to sleep and would be helping me tomorrow evening as well as Saturday. He knew this, but he needed to find a reason to storm out of the house again and hang out with his friends. He told me that he needed to be "with people who respected him," and out the door he went. He took my car keys, leaving me no transportation if I needed it. I was so used to this that I really didn't care at this point. The mess was cleaned up from his project, leaving me the chance to decorate and make the house look inviting again, and it wasn't worth the energy to fight. He left, and I went to bed.

Saturday morning came, and I was busy trying to tidy up for tomorrow's special day. I spent all day at my dad's home as I was still without a washer. It's been over six weeks at this point, and running back and forth to either my dad's or to the Laundromat was getting old. I helped my dad decorate the cake that he made for his first great-grandchild, which was simply beautiful. It was a white and pink tier cake, and around the second tier, pink flowers adorned his creative masterpiece. The cake topper displayed a baby in her cradle.

LOVE TURNED TO HATE

It was perfect! It was created with love, which made the cake even more special.

I loaded up the car with all the clean clothes and food (homemade meatballs and sauce, German potato salad) that my dad worked all day preparing. I headed home to continue cleaning and setting up for the big day. Upon my arrival home, my husband was sitting in his chair watching TV. As I pulled up to the house, other people were stopping by with items they had made. They helped me unload the things from my car and commented as to why my husband was just sitting there and not offering to help. I immediately commented that "I am used to this," to which the reply back was, "This isn't right." I agreed that it wasn't right but begged them not to say anything because his wrath was far worse than the additional work that I had to do.

Everyone dropped off the items, helped me put them away, and then left. I am sure the coldness in the room, which was the atmosphere my husband displayed, made everyone feel so uncomfortable that they felt it best to just go. One friend stayed to go over the finishing touches, making sure that nothing was forgotten. With that, my husband yelled to me that he was hungry and it was my job to get him something to eat *now*. I looked at him, annoyed, as it was embarrassing to have him humiliate me in front of company, and he gave me a glare that I knew I was in for a round of trouble.

Rather than being humiliated again, I thanked my friend, assuring her that I was fine. Things were beginning to change again as I now noticed that he didn't care if anyone else was around to hear him belittle me, whereas in the past, he would only do it in front of my children or me.

When she left, he started in on me with "it's my job to feed him" and how I better get him food. I had it! Maybe because I was tired from washing, cooking, cleaning, but I let loose on him. I told him, "Who do you think you are? You have no business talking to me like that. Are you happy that you embarrassed me again? What is wrong with you?"

I went into the kitchen fuming mad and proceeded to take the homemade meatballs that my dad cooked and made him a hot meatball sandwich. When I gave him the sandwich, he reprimanded me yet again that "this is a poor excuse for a dinner, and it was not hot." Now in the past, every time that I made something for him, he would always complain that it was too hot, so this time, I carefully watched the time and made sure that it was lukewarm. He got up from his recliner in the living room and smashed the sandwich with his boot deeply into the newly laid carpet. As the children witnessed this, they quickly ran into the kitchen and grabbed the carpet cleaner and desperately tried to get these deeply embedded pieces of meatball and stains out of the carpet. Unfortunately, the stain was there, so the only thing I could do was push the chair over it. Just another reminder when I would look at it of the mess I made of my life.

The phone rang, and it was my friend asking me about the turkey that I was also having for the party. I quickly pulled myself together so I could answer the phone. He heard the phone ring, put the TV on mute and shouted loudly, "Who is it? I'll go in the other room and pick up the damn phone to see who you are talking to, you bitch."

I replied, "Go ahead."

He opted not to get on the other end but instead continued with his ranting. He then got up, ripped the phone out of my hand, and slammed the phone down. He pushed the items that were on the desk onto the floor, and I called him an asshole. He told me if I ever name-called him again, he would kill me. He stormed into the bedroom, took the baskets of neatly folded clean clothes that I had spent six hours doing with my father's help, and dumped them all over the bedroom floor. He went into the kitchen and made himself a cup of coffee, but instead of drinking it, as I thought that was what he was going to do, what any normal person would have done, he heaved it at me instead. The hot coffee struck the kitchen cabinet and crashed on the floor. Hot coffee was running down the cabinet and the walls.

I couldn't believe it, and with the look of shock on my face, speechless, he yelled, "Now you have something to do, you bitch, so get busy and clean it up because that's about all you are good for." He proceeded into the living room and headed straight toward the lamp, which was on the end table, smashing it as he tossed it to the ground, leaving broken glass embedded in the stained carpet for me to try and clean up. He yelled, "Now, bitch, clean it up," and made his exit for the door.

As he was leaving, a friend was entering, carrying in more food for the party, and she yelled to him, "What is wrong with you?"

And so the task of redoing what had already been done began. For the first time in my life, I thanked God that my mother and Nanny weren't alive to witness what had just happened, and I dried the tears from my eyes and proceeded to try and clean up the stain in the new carpet, which had just been laid the day before. I cried for a long time that night and just longed to be free—free from this man and his tirades. What did I ever do in this life to deserve this treatment? What had he reduced me to? How was I ever going to be able to live my life normally? How much more could I take?

All these questions poured through my mind as I scrubbed, cooked, and tried to hold it together. It felt like I was beginning to lose my mind. I knew that I deserved happiness, peace, and love, and it wasn't going to be found with this tyrant.

Before leaving for the night after his rampage, he quickly reminded me with his threat that if anyone says one word to him and he feels that they know what he has done to me, he will go into his shed and grab a weapon (tool) and start smashing heads. He said he will greet people with, "Hello, you f—ing assholes, welcome to my house." I was told that I had to treat him with respect and do as he said, or he would cause so many problems at this affair. He would embarrass me like I have never been embarrassed before. I knew that these weren't idle threats, and so I did as I was told. What a way to plan for a fun event, constantly worrying what he would do and if he would show up.

Earlier in the week, he smashed the wooden mallard duck that I had on the table from my Nanny. The wooden duck landed on the floor, causing the neck and beak to break. I was so upset over him destroying the gift I had received from Nanny because it was irreplaceable. My Nanny was deceased, and so that duck, as silly as some may feel this is, meant more to me than I can say. This is what he does, destroys things that hold a special place in my heart and memories.

I could feel that I was beginning to crack, just like the items that he destroyed, and I wondered how much more of this I could take before there was no turning back. I started to believe that you can't have both, a happy childhood and a happy adulthood. I had the best childhood, and my poor children were being denied theirs. I just wanted to give them what I had, and I was failing miserably. I went to the one place where I could cry and not be heard, in the shower, and there I let it all out. This was my place of release as I didn't turn to drugs or alcohol. I knew I always needed to have a level and clear head if I was going to survive.

Over the years, he has broken things that the children had made for me for the holidays, the things that hold a sentimental value because they were made by my children. I think the reason he chooses to break things that mean so much to me are because years ago, the first time that he struck me, I hit him back so hard and promised if he ever laid a hand on me again, he'd live to regret it. He was quick to inform me that if I didn't wise up, he would take his truck and run it through my front window. He said if I thought that I was going to have everything and he would have nothing, he would see to it that I had nothing because he would kill me. Some might think these were idle threats, but after years being with this man, I knew he meant every word he said.

I worried all the while that I was getting dressed and ready to head out to church for the Christening. He was home at the time and annoyed that I didn't invite his family, but I did, and his mother wasn't feeling well enough for the drive down. He continued to berate me and tell me how wrong I was because he felt his family should be there too. With that, he informed me that he would not be going to the baptism nor would he be attending the party afterward. His excuse was if his family wasn't coming, then he wouldn't be there either.

I hoped he meant what he said because I had to leave for the church, and I left him drinking his coffee. I prayed so hard in church that I wouldn't be coming home to a mess and face that humiliation as I did the day before and that he would do as he said and be out of the house. When the family and I pulled up to the house, the truck was gone, so I knew it was going to be a good day. I thanked God for answering my prayers and decided I was going to enjoy this day and celebrate.

It turned out to be a lovely day. Family and friends were laughing and enjoying each other's company. The house was filled with lots of love and laughter, something that had been missing for some time now. I was lost in that moment and wished it could go on forever.

The happy, carefree day soon was over when he arrived home later that evening. There were a few family members still at the house, and when he entered, he walked right past everyone, said not a word, and went into the kitchen. He grabbed some food, sat down, and ate, not saying a thing. Although it was rude, I would rather him be rude than to have said more nasty things to my family or me.

When the last of the guests left and I began to clean up, he commented that he deliberately did not show up for the Christening, and now everyone knows what a bitch I am. I couldn't figure out where he got this idea from or even if it made any sense, but I certainly wasn't about to ask any questions. I was exhausted and headed upstairs to get my shower and then sleep on the sofa as I had work the following day, and I couldn't deal with anymore of his nonsense. I closed my eyes, thanking God for making my granddaughter's christening so special.

The alarm went off for him the following morning, and as he got ready for work, he couldn't find what he was looking for, so he loudly started yelling and woke us up. He ransacked the clothes basket, tore apart the dirty laundry, and located the shirt he wanted to wear that day! Needless to say, it was dirty, and that enraged him once again. I was called all kinds of nasty names and accused of deliberately choosing not to do his laundry and I was being spiteful. Well, maybe if he had the washer connected, I would be able to do the wash daily like I used to do, but he disconnected the washer, and so I had to do my wash on the weekends and spend hours upon hours either at my father's house or at the Laundromat to get everything done. It was him that disconnected the washer, and it was only supposed to be for three days, and I am going on four weeks without a washer. So whose fault is it, I might ask. But no, it was my fault, and I bore the wrath of this insane human being.

Thank God he would be over the road for a few days. I needed that quiet time to get my thoughts and strength back to fight this ugly giant that I am living with. After work and after helping the kids with homework, I headed to the Laundromat to get all the wash finished. At this point, I believe he is now delaying the completion of the bathroom and hooking up the washer on purpose. It is just another way to punish me and put me in my place as he told me over and over again, "I'm a woman, and it is my job to make my man happy…cooking, cleaning, and having sex when he wants it." What era did this guy come from?

Attending the girls' softball games was always fun. I enjoyed being on the cheering squad at their games. It was good quality time that we girls had together. My life was normal there, filled with laughter and good times. Grabbing a hoagie, cheesesteak, slice of pizza for dinner was the best! Heading to the ice cream stand was the icing on the cake. If he were home, this wouldn't do, and the kitchen slave (me) would be busy cooking and cleaning until it was time for bed. I was just like the kids on these nights, loving every minute of it.

While enjoying a show on TV, the sound of the truck pulling into the driveway made us all uneasy. The girls quickly ran upstairs to their rooms to avoid him. I on the other hand had no place to run. He entered, said hello, and headed right for the TV, changing the channel and sitting in his chair. He never cared what we were watching; it really didn't matter because we were girls, and in his mind, girls didn't matter. He took the remote control and changed the TV channel with no consideration for what I might be watching.

As much as this got under my skin, I remained quiet because there was no TV show that was worth listening to him scream or being struck or kicked. He had few words to say, which was unusual, and so I said good night and headed for the bedroom to go to sleep. My youngest daughter crept down the stairs and came into the bedroom to be with me. She was scared, now that he was back, and so she came to lie beside me. I had planned on carrying her back to her room once she fell asleep, but I was so tired that I slipped off to sleep myself.

When he was finished watching his shows on TV, he came into the bedroom, and upon seeing her in bed, he went wild. He had a lit cigarette in his hand, which he threw on the bed. He began his ranting and raving, which saved my daughter and me, or the mattress would have gone up in blazes with us in it. My youngest daughter grabbed the lit cigarette and got water to make sure nothing was festering in the mattress.

While doing that, he grabbed my legs, pulled me out of the bed onto the floor, and with his heavy work boots began kicking me in the back and in my ribs, cursing me for having her in bed. All the noise woke up everyone else in the household, and what had been a quiet, peaceful day turned into a nightmare.

I was badly hurt but I refused to let him see the pain that my body endured. I got up and went into the living room to sleep on the couch. I took some Tylenol for the pain and used a heating pad to help with my aching back. I grabbed my inhaler to assist me in breathing as the cigarette smoke made breathing difficult due to my asthma, and now having sore ribs from the kicking made my ability to breathe even worse. I was struggling for each and every breath. As for him, he thought nothing of what he had just done to me, and he simply just slipped into bed and fell asleep.

Work was difficult with the pain in my ribs, but I couldn't miss work as we needed the money, and I didn't want to be home if there was even the slightest chance that he'd be there. Fortunately for us all, he had a long haul over the road, and he'd be gone for a week or so. On the other hand, that meant it would be another week before we would have our washer hooked up and our heater. If I had the money, I would have paid someone to complete the job, but I didn't, and so we waited for him. It was getting closer to the end of fall now, and the heater would soon be needed as well as the shower enclosure being brought inside and hooked up before the cold set in. It was becoming tiring and annoying to have to come home from work only to go out again to do the laundry. With six people, there is always a lot of wash, but since it was me who was being inconvenienced and not him, it didn't matter.

The following couple of days, every time I took a deep breath, my back hurt, but I was afraid to go to the doctor's or the hospital for fear that a report would be taken, and I would suffer at his hands once again. Eventually, the pain lessened. Had I been assured that he would never be permitted back in the house or anywhere near us, I would have gladly driven myself to the hospital, but I knew that everything is a process, and with my luck, he would have returned, and it wouldn't be a few broken ribs this time; he would succeed in killing me. My broken ribs were confirmed when I went for my yearly mammogram. The break caused a shadow on the mammogram, which had to be checked by the Doctor, who then asked if I remembered ever fracturing my ribs. I, of course, did not confirm how or when this happened. I just let it go.

It soon became obvious to me that the only happy times in my life were when he was over the road for long periods of time. I only wished that he would be man enough to say that he wanted out of this marriage and leave, but that wasn't happening. He believed he was right and I was wrong and that sooner or later, he would break me into being a good wife. He handed me a piece of paper, which read, "How to Be a Good Wife," which was written in the 1950's. I thought it was a joke and started laughing. He said seriously, "Read it and learn! This is the way it should be."

I just shook my head in disbelief. I really am living a nightmare. He proceeded to say that nothing more would be done in the house until I learned how a woman should treat her husband and begin acting accordingly. I would not be having the bathroom fixed, the heater fixed, the washer hooked back up. Nothing would get done until I followed the rules from the article on how to be a good wife. *Wow*, this man really is out of touch with reality!

The girls and I went to happy family functions without him as he was over the road a lot lately, or that's where he said he was, which made it possible for us to enjoy ourselves. I knew that I could make it on my own as a single mother and really believed that life would be much better without all this stress and abuse. I began putting money away so that I could seek legal counsel and find a way to end this torture.

The sound of the truck could be heard pulling in the driveway after close to a week of peace and quiet. Who would enter the door was always questionable. It was late, and I was just getting ready for bed. He walked into the bedroom, asked where a piece of paper was that he couldn't locate that he claimed he had put inside an empty cigarette package. I told him that I didn't see it and that all the empty cigarette packs that I had seen were still on top of the refrigerator. He told me that they weren't and yelled at the top of his lungs, that I was a "f—ing liar."

Back, he stomped into the bedroom where I was now quickly and nervously putting away the clothes since I didn't need him to rant and rave over why his clothes weren't put away, when he noticed a full glass of ice tea that I had poured for myself on the bureau. He grabbed the glass of ice tea, dumped it out all over my papers and clean clothes. The drawer had been open as I was putting away clothes, so the ice tea dripped inside the bureau drawer and all down the front of the bureau. Then he took the remainder of the ice tea and poured it upside down on the carpet. He yelled obscenities toward me and left.

So once again, after a busy day at work, what I thought would be an easy night simply putting the wash away turned into a major project. I now had to scrub the bureau, empty the drawers, and scrub inside each one, rewash all the clothes yet again at the Laundromat that I just did along with the ones that were in the bureau, and then scrub the carpet. So much for getting to bed early.

This relationship was like living a reoccurring nightmare. You never knew what triggers would set this man off. A simple thing, like not having dinner ready the minute he came through the door from work, was enough to cause him to throw a hot coffee cup at me and then demand that I get on my hands and knees to clean up the mess that *he* made. In the early stages of this abuse, I would tell him, "No," but I soon learned to keep my mouth shut.

When I talked back, I was hit, kicked, smacked, and pushed. It didn't take long for me to figure out how to avoid the pain of being struck, so cleaning up his mess or simply following his commands meant I would be saved another day from his violent outbursts. These outbursts and violent acts were becoming increasingly more frequent. Sadly, this is something that all abused people learn quickly. In order to survive, I needed to remain quiet and do as I was told. I realize today that I lost my voice, my freedom, because I had children that I needed to protect at all costs, and so I did as I was told. I would rather his abuse be directed at me and not my kids, and so I just did as I was told.

Valuable tips that I learned from living with this man to protect myself were: it is not important to be right at the cost of losing your life; it is better to be quiet and hopefully defuse the situation. I could think a lot, curse him in my head, but my mouth needed to stay closed. This was a huge task for me to learn and apply as I am not one to sit back and say nothing, nor am I one to be bullied; but in this situation, I quickly learned how to play the game if I wanted to stay alive.

Weeks passed, as did the storm, so when we got an invite to see his parents in New York, I foolishly thought this would be a pleasant trip for the family, and so I agreed to go. The kids all wanted to go, and so I thought why not. Things were calm there on the home front, so I felt pretty safe that this trip just might be a pleasant getaway, and so I packed the family up, and we headed out to see his folks.

Along the way, that switch went off in his brain, and because I asked a simple question (to this day, I can't remember exactly what it was, probably how much farther it was to his folks), he went crazy and started yelling at me, hitting me, and calling me all kinds of vulgar names. The girls were in the back seat yelling at him to stop it. We were traveling on a superhighway when he took his foot off the gas pedal, kicked me with his boot, and reached over and opened my door. The car was swaying across the lanes as he tried with all his might to push me out onto the superhighway, and I was holding onto the door handle with every bit of strength that I had left. The door shut on my hand, which meant I let go of the door. He then took his foot off me and continued to drive. He told me that he could have gotten rid of me right then and there, so I had better watch myself, because if I ever thought about taking his kids away from him, this would be how I'd end up—dead.

My body ached from being kicked and the door slamming on my hand, but I was alive and not laying out there on the highway. My kids were safe in the back seat, shaken up badly but safe. We then were given the lecture that none of this was to be mentioned when we arrived at his parents' home. I was terrified, and I can only imagine how the girls felt. We were now going to an unfamiliar area where I basically knew no one except for his parents, which was frightening, with a man whom I felt was certifiably crazy.

When we arrived, I begged the girls to say nothing because I was afraid of what he would do. There was no one that I could speak to as these were his parents and his family, and I was the outsider, so all I could do was hope and pray that the weekend ended quickly with no incidents. It is honestly a very frightening experience to watch someone go from being out of control back to normal in a matter of a few minutes. Never would I believe it if someone told me this was possible until I witnessed this firsthand. This man could easily have ended my life right in front of our children and thought nothing of it.

That night, when I got into my nightgown, the bruises were clearly on my back and rib area, and my hand was black and blue where the door closed on it. My body was throbbing with pain, and then to make matters worse, he forced himself on me. I begged him to leave me alone. I said, "No" over and over again, and all he could do was laugh and tell me I was his, and he would do as he pleased. He tore my clothes off and violently raped me. I was crying, and he didn't stop. Tears were flowing down my checks onto my pillow, and he continued to satisfy his needs. I prayed to God to make this end soon. I never felt so violated.

When he was through, he rolled over and went to sleep. I got up, showered, and cried so hard that my eyes were all puffy the next day, and I had to say that it was from allergies when his family asked. God, how I detest this man.

Who would ever think that I would be in a situation such as this? Having led a sheltered life, a life filled with love, encouragement, happiness—to end up here is simply unthinkable. But here is where I was, and I needed to be cautious and on my guard if I was to stay alive and protect my precious children. If only I had the money to get out of this situation, I would have been gone a long time ago, but without money, I was a prisoner, and I had to save until that time when I could finally find a way out of this horrific nightmare that I was living.

When we arrived home safe and sound, as soon as he left for work, I contacted the phone company because he had threatened to cut the phone lines so that I had no way of calling for help. He said he could call them, and they would disconnect the phones just with his call. Well, the phones were in my name, and so I spoke to someone in their security department and told them of my fears, his threats, and his abuse. I was given a security code that only I knew, and they said that he would never be able to disconnect the phones without that code. They gave me some additional advice on how to protect myself and advised me to speak to the police, which I did.

I also notified and met with two lovely ladies from A Woman's Place, who offered my family and me a safe haven should we ever need it. We went to weekly meetings; the girls spoke to counselors that were trained to help children, while I spoke to counselors for adults, along with other women in similar situations as I. It was here that I learned his abuse was not my fault and that I wasn't to blame for his actions. I also learned how I could work on getting out of this deadly relationship. The signs of an abusive person fit him to a T. I was the victim of physical abuse, mental abuse, sexual abuse, and property/economic abuse. I was the poster woman for abusive relationships.

Physical abuse, I was taught, involved hitting, slapping, shoving, kicking, punching, burning, choking, not being allowed to leave home, use of objects to cause injury. Mental abuse was the threats, telling me what I could or could not do, name calling, and using words that hurt. Sexual abuse was the unwanted touching, forcing me to have sex against my will, and telling him no when he did as he pleased. Property or Economic abuse was his stealing and destroying my personal belongings, taking money, and refusing the basic needs for the family (denying us hot water, heat, and food). I learned, to my shock, that I encounter all four forms of abuse and that I needed to get away from this man as soon as possible. I learned how to clear my head and stop blaming myself for being in this situation, that it was *not* my fault that he was the way that he was, and I gained the strength and support to make the move and turn this life of mine around.

He fit the definition of an abuser in all categories. By definition the abuser is typically charming, jealous, manipulative, controlling (constant checking your whereabouts), a victim (always someone else's fault), narcissistic (whole world revolves around him and his needs), inconsistent (mood swings—happy one minute, angry the next), critical, disconnected (isolation from family and friends to force you into total submission), hypersensitive (slightest offense sends him ranting), vicious and cruel, and finally insincerely repentant. It was a scary moment when I came to realize that each category fit him to a T and that I was actually living with a full-fledged abuser. He needed the help, and I needed to end this relationship.

All the things his first wife said to me after I married him rang in my ears over and over again, and I began to believe all the horrible stories that she confided in me that he did to her. We both were his punching bags, his victims, and we both were intelligent women, so how could we have fallen for this man? What didn't we see when we married him or even dated him? I still question that to this day. How could I have been so stupid?

Once again, he left for an over-the-road trip, which meant he'd be gone for days, possibly a week. Peace at last! The girls and my life went on peacefully for those few blessed days. We were able to go on fun outings, dine out when we chose, and/or sit and watch our favorite TV shows with no fear of being on pins and needles. Our turbulent life was filled with peace, if only briefly. It was a normal lifestyle, and normal felt wonderful! The simple pleasures to just enjoying time with the family and relaxing in each other's company were too few and far in between.

The following is excerpted from a 1950's high school home economics textbook.

How To Be A Good Wife

Have dinner ready. Plan ahead, even the night before, to have a delicious meal on time. This is a way of letting him know that you have been thinking about him and are concerned about his needs. Most men are hungry when they come home and a well prepared, warm meal is a warm welcome home.

Prepare yourself. Take fifteen minutes to rest so that you will be refreshed when he arrives. Touch up your make up, put a ribbon in your hair and be fresh looking. He has just been with a lot of work weary people. Be a little gay and a little more interesting. His boring day many need a lift.

Clear away the clutter. Make one last trip through the main part of the house just before your husband arrives, gathering up school books, toys, papers, etc. Then run a dust cloth over the tables. Your husband will feel he has reached a haven of rest and order and it will give him a lift.

Prepare the children. Take a few minutes to wash the children's hands and faces (if they are small), comb hair and, if necessary, change their clothes. They are little treasures and he would like to see them playing the part.

Minimize all noise. At the time of his arrival, eliminate all noise of the washer, dryer, dish-washer, or vacuum. Try to encourage the children to be quiet. Be happy to see him. Greet him with a warm smile and BE GLAD to see him.

Some don't: Don't greet him with problems and complaints. Don't complain if he is late for dinner. Count this as minor compared to what he might have been through that day.

Make him comfortable. Have him lean back in a comfortable chair or suggest that he lie down in the bedroom. Have a cool (or warm) drink ready for him. Arrange his pillow and offer to take off his shoes. Speak in a low, soft and pleasant voice. Allow him to relax and unwind.

Listen to him. You may have a dozen things to tell him, but the moment of his arrival is not the time. Let him speak first!

Make the evening his. Never complain if he does not take you out to dinner or to other pleasant entertainment. Instead, try to understand his world of strain and pressure, his need to unwind and relax.

THE GOAL: TRY TO MAKE YOUR HOME A PLACE OF PEACE AND ORDER WHERE YOUR HUSBAND CAN RELAX IN BODY AND SPIRIT.

Chapter 16

THE NEED TO GET OUT

"A healthy relationship doesn't drag you
down. It inspires you to be better."
—Mandy Hale

At this juncture of my life, I began to realize that I needed to do whatever it was to protect not only my children but myself as well. Where would they be without their mother? And after so many battles with this man, I realized that it was more important to just keep quiet and let him think that he was in charge, if I wanted to survive. I am not the type of person who allows others to push me around or say things without a comeback, but when you know that you could lose your life over it, you soon realize that it is better to just bear the insults and live another day.

Believe me, the thoughts that ran through my head were how I could get revenge on him for everything, and then my children's faces flashed before me, and I just let it go. Protecting my children and myself was foremost on my mind, and so if letting him think that he was the powerful one, then so be it. My strength, along with whatever fight I had left, was needed in a more positive and beneficial way, and that was escaping from this torture and surviving, and so my long journey to freedom begins.

His outburst ran in cycles. He may go four to six weeks where everything was fine, calm, and even happy, and then without warning, the flip side of him would surface, and there would be four to six weeks of rants and anger whenever he came home. It became a pattern, one that I was becoming all too familiar with. The good days soon turned into bad ones, and before I knew it, there were more bad than good. If I remained strong, he would just continue to destroy items, but when I would break down and cry, he would mellow and stop the rampage. It was as if he delighted in seeing me reduced to tears.

I believe he felt empowered when I cried. Words of comfort were not what came from his mouth; rather, it was always words of reprimand, blaming me for him becoming so angry. He was relentless with his hostility. Once the outbursts were through, he would leave the house, cursing on his way out the door to go wherever he wanted.

I later came to learn he had a girlfriend on the side, and this was his way to get out for a few hours to be with her. I honestly did not care. Maybe now he'd leave me alone. I found this out when the girlfriend's husband called me to tell me that my husband was cheating on me with his wife, who was cheating on him. Oh my God, what was happening? He wanted to catch them in the act and tear into my husband. I think the man thought that I would be upset about this relationship and my comeback was, "I feel sorry for you if you love your wife, but as for me, she can have him." That would have been a gift from above to be freed of him and all his tirades.

After the call, I began the process of cleaning up, and the sense of relief that he was gone took over. My children always came to the rescue, helping clean up from his destruction. I think the hurt from each outburst was worse when I had to watch them help me. I had instructed them every time they heard him yelling and destroying things to stay in their bedrooms, and if they heard him coming up the steps, to lock their doors, and if they had to climb out the window, do it and run to the neighbors for help, but do not try and fight him off. We drilled this over and over again like we drilled a fire drill. I needed to be positive that they understood the severity of what I was telling them if we were to survive. I was the one who made this terrible mistake by marrying him, and I should be the only one who paid the price, not my children.

My oldest daughter, much like her mother, would not listen when told to stay upstairs but would confront him over and over again. One time, when he was punching me, pulling my hair, she went up to him to get him away from me. He yelled in her face, so angry that the saliva from his mouth looked like a mad dog, and grabbed her hair, pulling out her earring. She, in turn, kicked him in his private area and ran. He was shocked that a *woman* would have the nerve to go up against him. He left the house to go to his friends because his pride was stripped from him at that very moment, and I told him I would kill him if he touched my daughter. My oldest daughter said she wasn't going to let him hurt me anymore.

How I wished I could just lock him out so that he could never enter this house again, but the law wouldn't allow it. The only way that things might change would be for me to file charges against him. I called and reported these outbursts, but all it ever did was make him angrier, and who paid the price in the end? Not him but the children and I. I had to endure these outbursts until I could get out and start fresh. The road ahead was not going to be an easy one.

Being a private person, it was a huge embarrassment having my neighbors see and listen to these horrific outbursts and witness these violent behaviors, but I had to put aside my pride and rely on their eyes and ears for my protection. The lawyer told me to begin a journal, documenting everything that occurred and file police reports after each incident. I had to build a case against him if I wanted to get a protection from abuse, which really is as good as the paper it is written on.

As for the house, it was in both names, and I couldn't, by law, throw him out. I couldn't even change the locks. It was so unfair. I paid for this house. I put the down payment, and I made the monthly payments, not him, and yet I can't throw this abuser out. It is so much easier for him to find a place as a single person than it would be for me with a family of five. I was also advised not to pack up and leave because he could call this desertion, and I would lose everything that I worked so hard for (the house). And so the struggles, along with the verbal and physical abuse, would continue until he gets so mad with his life that he leaves. What great news! Will that ever happen since this man thinks he is the man of the house, the one in charge?

I began putting some extra money into the account and wondered why I was having bounced check fees, especially since I put more money in there than was needed for the bills. I asked him about this as the bank said there were numerous withdrawals from the MAC machine. It came as no surprise that this infuriated him that I, a woman, had the nerve to question him, the man. He informed me that he took eighty dollars out of the account because it was *his* money. I said, "This was for the mortgage, and now where do you expect me to get the difference to cover the bounced checks?"

He said, "Oh, well, looks like you will be out on the street too." He continued with his rant saying, "If I can't live in this house, neither can you. If I am going to live in a room or an apartment, then you will be forced out of this house when it goes into foreclosure." He continued by calling me a "bitch" and telling me, "You'll pay."

After his ranting and raving, he simply sat down in his chair and turned on the TV as if nothing had just happened. Meanwhile, my insides are racing, and I am trying to find a way to get this mortgage paid. I learned a valuable lesson that day. I opened my own account the following day and put my "getaway money" into my account. A word to the wise: if you are in a tumultuous relationship as I was, you need to get your own account without him knowing and save every penny that you can. This life of mine was not going to be like this for much longer.

The bathroom was still unfinished, and we still had the same mess to deal with months later. Now on the bathroom door, he drew a skull, the symbol that you use to indicate something is poisonous, with black permanent maker. I asked him about it, and he just laughed, so I let it go. The floor was all torn up where all you saw was the dirt. It was a huge hole, waiting for the concrete to be poured. Our youngest daughter looked at the floor and asked her father why there was such a big hole in the bathroom, and to both of our surprise, his response was, "This is where I am going to bury your mother." She screamed, and fear took over us both once more. He thought it was funny. He thought it was a joke, but I felt differently and knew that this man was crazy enough to do just what he said.

He shut the door and went into the living room to watch TV with no remorse for what he just said or how upset our youngest child was by his remarks. I pondered over this and decided that I needed to take some photos before the floor was laid with concrete so that I would have proof in court. I did just that after he left for work and documented this in my journal, recounting the daily encounters of abuse, physical as well as mental and verbal. I needed to be prepared for this journey out of hell, leaving no stones unturned. I kept the journal locked in my car, and as I completed several pages, I would hide them at my parents' home in a sealed envelope in case something happened to me.

My dad was not aware of the contents of the envelopes that I asked him to hold on to until much later. He also was unaware of the abuse that I had been enduring as I didn't want to involve him or my brother. It was my responsibility to find a way out, and when the time was right, I would fill them in, but not now. I worried what my husband might do to them or to me as well as worrying what my dad and brother might do to my husband. It wasn't worth ruining their lives for a horrible mistake that I had made. My long journey toward freedom was underway, and *I was in charge!*

The bathroom scenario was haunting me as it was my daughter. She would not go past the bathroom door without someone being with her, and she never let me out of her sight. This poor child was being tortured by something that her father said, and he continued to say, "It was just a joke." Seeing the fear and pain, I made an appointment for her to talk to someone along with her sisters. Seeking professional help was the wisest decision I made, not only for the children but for myself as well. I realized that we needed help, and I couldn't do it on my own.

The children and I continued to attend meetings every week, sometimes more, and I felt safe knowing that I found someone, someplace where I was safe and could speak without being judged. My girls were able to talk to other children who were feeling the same pain that they were feeling, and no longer did they feel alone. They could talk about what they were thinking as well as put their thoughts down on paper. It was a healing process. It was a safe meeting place, and we knew that if ever we were in harm's way, we could seek refuge there. We couldn't let their father know what we were doing or where we were going. We made an agreement with one another, and we kept that pact. We were on our way to a better life. The road was a long one, and we had many more rocky roads ahead of us, but we were starting out on this journey together, and we weren't stopping now until we were all safe and happy again.

Upon his return later that evening, as if what he had done earlier wasn't enough, he continued on with his rampage, telling me that he gets no respect here at home with all women, and how we should respect him. He went on and on, and I turned him off in my head. I don't know what else he was yelling, but I blocked him in my head. He mumbled some more words and then left for the living room and turned on the TV. I went to bed and tried to sleep.

It was the same thing the following evening when he arrived home from work. He now was arguing because we had no money to purchase things he wanted or needed to work on the bathroom. He refused to listen when I told him that we had the electric, water bill, and car insurance to pay. Instead of being an adult and understanding that these are normal monthly bills, and sometimes we have to wait until we can buy things that would be considered nonessential, he accused me of being stupid and unable to handle money.

Try as I may to explain to him that by him being self-employed now, it would take some time to catch up, as he wasn't bringing that much of an income home. Well, that infuriated him again, and he called me an "asshole", and reminded me that he was the male, head of household, and what he says goes. Funny, but I certainly am not the male head of household, but I am bringing in the steady income and paying the bills, so when I say we don't have the money to do what he wants to do, it is true. These daily encounters with him were eating me up inside. The only thing that kept me sane and staying strong was knowing that *I would get out of this situation.*

Evening after evening, he would come home with another suggestion for how this marriage could work, and it all involved me. He told me to make a list of all the things that bothered me about him, and when I couldn't (wouldn't) present the list, he was annoyed and said I didn't care. Why would I ever compile a list stating the many things that bothered me about him when the end result could be another beating or even my death? What kind of fool did he think I was? He asked why we aren't going back to counselling, to which I replied, "I told you why. We went to counselling, and you complained that it was a woman, and she was only on my side, always siding with me.

"She said marriage was fifty-fifty, and when she spoke to you about your attitude, you flared up and told her you weren't going anymore. Why then would I try to seek counselling again when you are right and everyone else is wrong? I am finished with counselling."

I am reminded him that I was sick and tired of being told how to be a better woman/wife and what my wifely duties are. He yelled and yelled and yelled some more and then told me he was leaving. He asked for a suitcase, to which I replied, "We don't have one." He stormed into the bedroom, gathered some clothes, and quickly informed me that he contacted his payroll department to do a direct deposit into his new account with his name on it only, and that he will not be giving me a dime. I let him rant because I knew differently and that he would have to support his two girls. All I wanted was to see him leave.

The ranting continued with, "Before I'll pay you any more, I will become indigent. Let's see how you survive now without my money. I need all the money I can get to set myself up, you f— bitch." He gathered up some of his belongings, and looking me in the eye, he yelled, "Go ahead and drop dead. That would save us all. I tell you this, Debbie, you will be lonely, you will regret this, and you will pay."

"Oh, and by the way, you know that before I leave, I'll have to break something! One other word of advice to you is don't you ever stand in the way of me seeing my kids, or so help me God, I will kill you. You are just another person whose grave I will piss on when you are gone."

I sat in the chair in the dining room, and my knees were shaking; they were so weak. I was more terrified of him than ever before as this anger was so intense that I honestly felt my life would end tonight. He walked out the door, carried his clothes, came back, yelled some more nasty comments to me, and then smashed out the first front window with his attaché case.

I screamed as I wasn't sure what was broken. I thought at first it was the TV screen. And the next thing I knew, he smashed out the second front window. He screamed into the front door, "If you want me to fix the window, I will be at my friend's house since I can't live here, you bitch. But you know what you'll have to do to get me back home to fix these windows." He always made reference to sex as the price I had to pay to get anything done around the house, and that was not going to happen if it meant I had to learn how to do it myself.

His final remark was, "When you call and say you are sorry and ready to be a wife, you know where you'll find me." With that he got into his truck and drove off with such haste that he burnt rubber as all my neighbors stood and watched.

As soon as he left, neighbors ran over to help me clean up the mess and calm me down. The two younger girls were around the corner with their friends playing, and when they came home, they were in shock. My neighbors boarded up the two windows and ordered new replacement windows for me, took my children over to their home for dinner, and helped them with their homework as one neighbor sat with me, trying to calm me down. It was just another nightmare from hell, but it was getting worse with each incident. I called the police to have the report on file, and the officer gave me some hotlines to call in an emergency. I was told to seek a court order for protection from spousal abuse.

So embarrassing to be in this situation, I was mortified, and when I had the time to quietly think back on what the counselor from a Woman's Place told me—that domestic violence happens to anyone, no matter your income, race, religious beliefs, or even your level of education—I gathered up my pride again and was more determined to put an end to this chapter of my life.

Before leaving, he double bolted the outside shed where his tools were kept along with our kerosene heaters. He told me if I messed with his tools that I would pay. He said the next time, he would be around and drive his truck through my front windows. He reminded me over and over again that I would pay.

I slept on the floor in the family room because my bedroom was next to the living room, and I was afraid if he carried out his threat about driving through the front windows, I was in harm's way in my bedroom as well as in the living room. So I felt a little safer sleeping in the family room. I didn't go upstairs with the kids to sleep because I needed to be close to the door so that I could hear if he was coming in. I had placed a chair up against my front door for fear that he would return. It would make it more difficult for him to simply open the door this way.

I wasn't allowed to change the locks even after this stunt, and so the only thing that I could think to do was place a chair up underneath the doorknob, making it harder for him to gain entrance, and at least I'd hear him and be better prepared. My neighbors all said that they would be on the watch for him and his truck, and if he showed up, they would call 911.

Thank God for these people as I felt a lot safer knowing that everyone was watching out for my children and me. Everyone saw him in action and heard all the vile names he called me. I told the children that we would all be okay, that I wouldn't let anything happen to us. I gave them that assurance to help them sleep, but I certainly didn't believe it myself. I was a watchman that night, getting little to no sleep.

The alarm went off the next morning, and I got the girls ready for school and myself ready for work. Looking back on this, I really don't know how I managed to keep my sanity and composure throughout all of this.

As I went over to the desk to gather up the bills and see which ones I could pay with this week's paycheck, I came across something very interesting. On the calendar, my soon-to-be ex-husband had marked under the date 9/29 in his handwriting, "Leaving." I wondered how long he had been planning this. Was this his ploy to exit, or did I mess up his plans by having him leave a few days before his scheduled time? I find it very strange that he would have written on his calendar leaving if in fact he was so concerned about saving this marriage. It just struck me as being odd. He also had been searching for rooms to rent and even went out to check a few earlier in the week, based on the notes he had written on the calendar.

Don't get me wrong, I am happy that he chose to leave when he did. The date of his departure didn't matter to me. My fear heightened when he left because I knew that the most lethal time in an abusive relationship is after you leave, and in this case, it was him who left. It was an extremely dangerous time, and I was honestly scared to death of him.

The following day, I received a phone call from his attorney, which in fact was his brother's attorney and someone that I had met before. He said that this was really difficult for him as he knew both my husband and me, but he needed to talk to me about what my husband did last night, his violent outbursts, and how sorry he was for this and that he still loved me and wanted to work things out. The attorney was asking me to give my husband another chance, to which I quickly replied, "If this was his way of showing how he loved me, then I'd be better off if he hated me."

I informed his attorney that I along with the children have been living under a great deal of pressure with these violent outbursts, and I have no intentions of working things out with his client. His actions spoke volumes, and his words meant nothing. I told him to go ahead with the divorce proceedings and that I would be getting my own attorney.

Later that evening, my husband's friend, who had been helping him with the reconstruction of the oil burner, stopped over to see how we were, which I appreciated. He offered to put the oil burner back together for me since the weather was changing, and we would be in need of heat soon. I told him I would pay him for his time, but he wouldn't accept the money. I was grateful that he was doing this as I knew my dad and brother knew nothing about oil burners living in the city, but they could get the bathroom back in shape as my brother had his own home improvement business. I knew that the time had come to fill both my dad and brother in on what was happening. It had been something that I had hoped I could spare my dad from ever hearing.

Chapter 17

THE SHAME OF IT ALL

The scars you can't see are the hardest to heal.
　　　　　　　　　　　　　　　　—Curiano

I called my dad and my brother and let them know briefly the situation that I was left in; bathroom all torn apart, shower enclosure still in the backyard, no washer hookup, and the floor in the bathroom all dirt waiting on concrete. I cried and cried as this was my first release with my dad after all these many years of torture. Both my dad and my brother came up the next day and began making changes to the bathroom. The outer wall had to be opened to be able to place the new shower enclosure indoors and then sealed.

Outside, the house needed to have new aluminum siding, which needed to be finished in a timely fashion as winter was fast approaching. The oil burner, which gives us heat, had not been completely overhauled, and that was a huge problem. My soon-to-be ex-husband's friend had to come and take the oil burner, along with the many pieces that make it run back to his shop. He then informed me that he had a paying customer who needed to have hot water this weekend while he did the job on that man's oil burner, so he had to pick up the temporary heating system, which gave us our hot water, to use on that job. Now my family was without heat and hot water Friday, Saturday, Sunday, and Monday. All the while, my soon-to-be ex had the comfort in his new apartment of having these luxuries, while he left his family without any of these necessities.

My dad and brother felt frustrated because there was nothing they could do about the heat and hot water when the oil burner had been removed as they were not familiar with the setup. They offered us to stay with them at their homes. My dad and brother finished up the bathroom; laying a new floor; doing the walls; and putting in a new sink, toilet, cabinet, and door. The transformation was amazing! No longer did we have to pass by the bathroom door with skull bones painted on it to get to the bedroom. I know that my daughters and I felt like a terrible curse had been lifted from us.

Once the oil burner was returned and functioning, giving us heat and hot water, we felt like this horrible cloud had finally been lifted. It had been a very long road to get to this point. Months and months of waiting, begging him to please finish what he had started, and leaving us in this condition was finally over. I am forever thankful for my family and his one friend who brought this horrible nightmare to an end. After experiencing this, I have very strong convictions that if you start something, you need to finish it and in a timely fashion. I usually ask before a project is started now, "How long will this take?" before agreeing to begin something new.

Since I still wasn't divorced from this man, he still came around to see the girls and continued to remove items from his shed in the back. I wished that I didn't have to be around when he dropped by, but I wasn't comfortable having the children there alone, and so my hell continued. He thought that he could drop by whenever he chose, and I was determined that this would not be the case. I was in charge once again, and so I notified my attorney, who in fact notified his attorney, that the freedom he once had in stopping by was now a thing of the past. He needed to have a schedule and follow it.

This did not go well with him. He still believed that he is the master, and he will not be told what he can or cannot do! I heard this over and over and over again. He looked for one thing after another as a reason to stop by. First, it was for the title to his truck, then it was his birth certificate, and then for furniture to set up his place. It became quite clear that every time he visited his brother and his brother's attorney, whom his brother was paying for, he would place more demands on me. When I didn't accommodate his wants and needs quickly enough, the name-calling resumed.

He felt he was entitled to all the furnishings necessary to furnish his apartment. His demands were the sofa from our family room, the recliner, two end tables, computer and chair for the computer, a bed, a table and hutch, a television set, along with pots, pans, dishes, silverware, linens, towels and personal hygiene items. What planet did this man come from? The nerve and gall of him is unbelievable! I just wanted him to go, and so I gave him the sofa and recliner, along with two end tables, but he was not getting a bed as the girls each had their own beds, nor was he getting the only table that we had to eat our meals on. As for the hutch and table, his aunt had given that to me many years ago, and I told him no. He called me white trash, a b—ch, and he couldn't wait until I was dead.

He continued to threaten me by saying, "You better have someone watching over this house all the time because I will come and take it." Like a child, he said that he was going to notify his attorney that I was refusing to help him and give him what he needed. He carried on and on and on over the computer, which belonged to the kids, and they were upset with his badgering me, so they told him to take it. Can you believe that a man, supposed to be a parent, would actually take his children's computer? Well he did, and he felt no guilt in doing it.

Sure enough, the following day, I received a phone call from his attorney questioning why I wasn't cooperating with him by giving him what he needed to start his life over. Are you kidding me? I informed his attorney of the following facts: the computer, table, and chair had been my father's, and he gave it to the girls to use for school; the sofa and chair had been my aunt's, and she gave it to me for the family room; the hutch and table were given to me by his aunt because she knew that I really loved it, and every time we were in her home, she would say that it was mine one day, and so when she moved, she gave it to me; and there wasn't an extra bed to be given as I have four daughters, and they all have their own beds. The sofa was a sofa bed so he could sleep on that. And as for the television set, no way; they were all individual gifts to the girls, and he had no right to demand they give them up. They already gave him the computer basically to shut him up. Since we are on the topic of what is right, where was he when he left us in the condition that he did without heat or hot water with a bathroom torn apart?

There was no comment from his attorney. I then told his attorney that his client was not permitted to freely come and go here anymore. Set up times and dates, or he will not gain entrance. I also informed his attorney that my neighbors have been asked to call the police whenever the truck is here longer than fifteen minutes, which is enough time to pull up and pick up his children for their visit. I strongly encouraged his attorney to take this seriously because my neighbors are looking out for the girls, and I and they will dial 911. I knew the backlash from my ex would be coming, but at this point in my life, I didn't care. I couldn't let him think for one minute that I was afraid of him, or he would take me down. I stood my grounds, and my neighbors called the police when his truck was here longer than fifteen minutes. It didn't take too many visits and calls to the police before he knew that I was serious.

It is funny to note that this so-called family heirloom that meant so much to him (table and hutch) has been sitting in our youngest daughter's garage for several years, and he has yet to pick it up, so how important and sentimental was this article of furniture?

The girls and I spent many weekends down at my dad's, where we enjoyed his company and some delicious meals. It was always a happy time being there and sitting out back at the picnic table just enjoying the peace and quiet. While the girls were busy doing their own thing, I had the time to talk to my dad and tell him how much I appreciated his advice, support, and most importantly his love.

As I recounted the horrific events that forever changed my life as well as my outlook, my father took me in his arms, tears rolling down both of our checks, and he promised me that this pain would be over. He held me tight, and I knew that all the shattered pieces of my life and physical pain that I had endured were over, and I was forever safe, that never again would anyone hurt me like my second husband did.

I knew, at last, that things were going to be okay. No more secrets! I had my Knight in shining armor to protect both my children and me and that I could face anything with my dad by my side. The road ahead was going to be brighter, and we were going to be okay.

Chapter 18

MOTHER'S DAY

From every wound there is a scar, and every
scar tells a story. A story that says, "I have
survived." Turn your wounds into wisdom.

—Unknown

It was Mother's Day, which was supposed to be a day spent with me, but since it was his weekend and he felt in charge, he decided that it would be his choice as to when I would see them. He came to take the girls out that morning, so when he pulled up, I simply asked that he bring them back early enough so that I could spend some time with them as we were going out to dinner. He laughed and took the girls.

Time passed, and the afternoon turned into the dinner hour and stills no girls. Now panic set in, and I honestly thought that he had taken them for good. I called and called, and when he finally answered, he said he was just around the corner. He pulled up in front of the house, and I walked toward the truck to get the girls. With that, he jumped out of the truck and grabbed me around the neck, tightening his hold as he attempted to choke me.

I pulled away from his grip and ran up my driveway toward the house. He caught me and smashed my head into my car window, which was parked in the driveway. I fell to the ground dazed, and as I was attempting to get back up with the help of a neighbor, he got back into his truck and sped up on the front lawn, tearing up the grass, heading directly toward me. I ran, and he continued to put his foot on the gas pedal. Our youngest daughter was standing with me—the one he scared with the bathroom skull, tossing the lit cigarette in the bed, the one who was always near me to protect me in her own little way—when the truck came inches from hitting both of us.

A neighbor from across the street flew to my aide, reached into the driver's side of the window, and steered the truck away from my daughter and me down the hill. Had it not been for these two people, my daughter and I would have died. My worst fears were coming true. He was serious when he said he wanted to kill me. He was determined to kill me; I was sure of it. I was taken to the hospital, treated, and released. The police took the report and made sure that I was okay before leaving. There was a warrant out for him, and after he spoke to his lawyer, he turned himself in.

This, of course, made the local newspaper, which was yet another form of embarrassment for someone who always led such a private life. It was so humiliating to be exposed this way. I felt so ashamed and such a fool, and at this moment, I could see how he was really starting to tear me down. I knew in my head that I had to remain vigilant and strong, but the constant abuse was starting to take a toll on me.

I had been his punching bag for way too long, but this incident was the worst. His lawyer contacted me the following day, again trying to make excuses for this behavior. I told him if this happened to his wife or his daughter, he wouldn't be saying these things. There is no excuse for anyone acting this way, none at all. I informed him that his client needs to stay far away from me and this house until I have my day in court.

This crazed man took away from me my freedom. I was scared to go out alone. I was always looking over my shoulder, jumped at every sound I heard. I worked several jobs, and he knew where I worked, so I had to ask coworkers to please follow me out of the building at night to be sure I made it safely to my car. Then on my way home, I had to call my daughters (eldest ones) and have them wait for me by the door, watching me as I got out of the car and ran up to the house. I was afraid to put the trash out at night for fear that he would be hiding and attack me. I froze whenever I saw him, and the sound of his voice on the answering machine sent chills down my spine. I was afraid to sit out at night with my neighbors on the warm summer nights for fear that he would drive down the street and not only hurt me but take his anger out on my neighbors as well.

Living in fear is really not living. I notified my children's school about his irrational behaviors and begged them not to release my children to him for fear for their safety. Their teachers were wonderful and protected my girls. Their classrooms were a safe haven for the children, and I felt safe, knowing they were in such caring and trusting hands. The children always had to check in with me, and I did the same for them. He left threatening voice mails on the phone about not keeping his kids from him or he'd kill me. I had to listen to this until I had my day in court. I had the Protection from Abuse (PFA) court order against him, but in all honesty, it was just a piece of paper. I had to protect myself, being vigilant and always looking over my shoulder. Nighttime was the scariest time of all for me.

As if his irrational behaviors weren't enough, I had to deal with his latest fling. She was as out of control as he was. The week before the Mother's Day incident, his new girlfriend drove down my street, got out of her car, and attempted to pour sugar in my gas tank. I just happened to hear a car stop out front, so I opened my front door and caught her red-handed in the act. I ran outside and chased her down the street before she was able to do any damage to my car. I memorized her license plate and called the police. Two police cars arrived, and I filed charges against her.

What she didn't realize was I wasn't fighting to have him back; she could have him. There was no need to try and make me angry or suffer any more than I already had. I had suffered enough living the life I lived with him. She could have him with no fight from me! So now, not only did I always have to be looking over my shoulder, worrying about him, I now had her to add to the list of people to be mindful of for my safety.

Chapter 19

THE LONG JOURNEY BEGINS

Stand up for yourself and your rights
as a human being. You are strong.
You are beautiful. And there is more
to life than walking on eggshells.
—Domestic Violence Survivor

The months that followed were turbulent. I filed criminal charges against a man that I married and thought loved me. How a man, whom you thought loved you, quickly turns against you—and worse yet, tries killing you—is unimaginable. It was mind-boggling, and I felt ashamed and foolish. Why didn't I get out sooner? All these questions that I had ran through my head over and over again. What would I have told someone else who lived this hell to do? One thing that I have learned is until you walk in that person's shoes, you have no idea what you would do.

I needed to pull myself together and rely on that strength that was my inheritance from the women in my life and fight as if my life depended on it because it did. No more feeling sorry for myself and the poor choice that I made. I didn't create this monster that I married, and I wasn't responsible for his actions. Right now, when I see myself in the mirror, I see a torn-down woman, a frightened woman, and a woman who feels hopeless. Then with each passing day on my own, something came over me, and I saw a determined woman who still had hopes and dreams yet to fulfill, and with the help of God, I was going to accomplish them.

My life was spared for a reason, and I was going to make the most of my second chance. I took control over this life that I had been given, and no one would ever take that away from me, *no one*. I came to realize that I am a survivor. I made it through all the years of abuse, and I am now going to make this life of mine worthwhile. I need to be a strong role model for my four daughters, hopefully one that they see is strong and doesn't let anything or anyone take her down. I want them to never be put in the situation that I was in.

There were many court dates that took up a great amount of time—divorce, custody, child support, and criminal. Each category had its own agenda, set of guidelines, and rules. They didn't blend into one another. I felt like I was living in Doylestown. I wasn't allowing my life or my children's lives to be placed in someone else's hands, and so although I had an attorney, I did my homework and set up binders for each hearing.

I kept a daily journal when the abuse began, making sure to note what was said, how he acted, and the phone calls. I took pictures of the damages he created, the condition of the bathroom, and copies of the police reports. I was not going to be questioned as to where the evidence was or asked, do you recall when this happened? I had my timeline, and I had my proof. I knew that this was going to be one heck of a battle, but I was fully armed and ready to win. I was fighting not only for myself and my daughters but for all the women who suffered at the hands of their abusers and were either unable to speak up or afraid to speak. I was their voice.

The courts had a legal library for anyone to use, which I did. I spent many hours in this room, surrounded by lawyers and reference books. I had no intentions of entering the courtroom unprepared. It was essential for me to be proactive and to leave nothing to chance. With my tablet and pen, I took down notes and copied case law where it could apply to my situation, read about the cases, learned the legal terminology, and studied how the process worked from beginning to end.

Often times, I was able to ask a lawyer or two for some guidance as to where to look. It was a daunting task, and many times I left with a violent headache. I wasn't sure how much more my mind could absorb on a topic that I really wasn't well versed in. All I knew was that I would not leave the fate of my children and me solely in the hands of the attorney. This was my life, my children's lives, and who better to protect them than me. The old saying is only a fool defends himself in court, and in many ways, that is true; however, I also believed that only a fool puts all their trust completely in the hands of their lawyer, no matter how good he/she may be. You were the one whom the outcome would affect, so it was you who needed to have your facts together.

I was paying a hefty sum of money to have legal representation for all of my hearings, and I also was putting in a huge amount of time and energy writing and researching what needed to be done. Together, my attorney and I made a dynamic team. I presented my attorney with what my concerns were and what outcome I desired. I gave him the tools to achieve this and reminded him that it was my life that he held in his hands during each case, and I wasn't leaving a thing to chance. He was amazed to see the amount of work and time that I put into my case, and would comment that I should be a lawyer. He stated that he had never seen someone with such organizational skills or someone who went through so much to pre-pare for their case. It was a nice compliment, especially coming from someone in the legal field. Now all I prayed for was that all this work would benefit my family and finally set us free.

Prior to appearing in court, it is customary for your attorney to go over the facts and help you to be prepared when questioned. It is more or less like a dress rehearsal. I decided that it would behoove me to familiarize myself about this process, and so I sat in the courtroom and listened to some other people's cases, taking notes on how they handled it and what type of questions were being asked.

There were people from all walks of life, whose lives were being affected in one way or another. I came to realize that I wasn't alone. Lives were changing right before my eyes; emotions were high, and the judge, who sat up higher than the rest of us, was determining our fate. Tears, anger, sadness, and joy echoed in this cold and bar-ren room. The loud sound when the judge's gavel came down with a final decision was deafening. My heart was pounding; my palms were sweating as one case after another was heard, and one life after another was forever changed. Soon, it would be my turn to discover just what my fate would be. It was a nerve-wrecking experience, and all that consumed me now was fear.

In the hallways, lawyers in their expensive suits with their expensive attaché cases were busy advising their clients, while nervous chattering echoed throughout, and I knew my turn before the judge was quickly approaching. I had to get my mind in the right place, remove this fear, and replace it with confidence! I kept saying repeatedly a quote from Eleanor Roosevelt that my dad had given me, which was, "No one can make you feel inferior without your consent." I believed this, and the time had now come to put these words into action.

Dressed professionally, standing tall, I entered the courtroom, ready to defend myself. That's not to say that my knees weren't knocking, my hands shaking, and my mouth parched. I was more than scared; I was petrified, but this was my one and only chance, and I was ready. Fear had no place here today. Having my lawyer beside me was a huge advantage also because he could say what I was not permitted to refute in court.

There were no smiley faces to greet you, no comfy feeling that surrounded you in this room. It was all business. There on the right-hand side was the man I had married, whose love for me quickly turned to hate, along with his attorney. Our eyes met, and I quickly turned away from his glare. I needed to remain focused, strong, and confident, and so I reminded myself that no longer was he a loving man; rather, I was now sitting across from my abuser.

So many different emotions ran through me—fear, nerves, nauseous, anger, determination, and even a sense of optimism that things were about to turn around for me, and they would all be for the best. My older daughters were there for moral support, and I would occasionally glance back to where they were sitting and look into their eyes. That was the defining moment when I knew I needed to be here if I ever hoped to be able to move forward. I continually kept talking to myself in my head, telling myself to remain calm, be proactive, and uncompromising when it came to fighting for my freedom.

I was called to take the stand. I stood up, and with all the strength that I could muster in my body, I walked forward to take the stand. I placed my hand on the Bible, and I swore to tell the truth, the whole truth, and nothing but the truth, so help me God. I realized at that precise moment when my hand rested on the Bible that I was not alone in this battle. I felt God and my two angels (my mother and Nanny) standing right beside me, and I knew that I would remain strong and able to conquer this moment. No longer would I be voiceless at the hands of my abuser. The courts gave me my voice again, and I was going to use it to free myself from so many years of torture.

I didn't need to worry about the repercussions anymore. No more beatings, broken ribs, pushing, kicking, punches, hot coffee tossed at me, lite cigarettes tossed at me, name-calling being slung at me, and being embarrassed. *No more!* Today ended this for me as I found my safe haven, and I was going to use it. I was empowered with the truth.

Looking up at the judge, who sat so much higher than me, was intimidating, probably designed this way to make a person feel inferior; and then standing in front of me, his lawyer, who also tried to make me crumble, made me that much stronger. This was my fight, and by God, I was going to give it all I had. I was through being held down.

As his lawyer directed one question after another at me, I remained diplomatic and posed in my delivery as well as unwavering. He wasn't going to make this abuse appear like a lover's spat or lessen my pain. He tried twisting what I said to benefit his client, and I respectfully came right back at him, clearly stating, "That's not what I said. Don't twist my words!"

At one point, when asked a question, I took off with my answer, giving more details than he wanted or even expected, which opened the door for my attorney to further question the abuse and leave the judge with a clearer picture of exactly what life had been like for so many years.

I felt empowered with the truth. He was the one who had something to be afraid of. I was optimistic that the judge listened to my ex and then listened to me and in between found the truth. I felt confident that I had done all that was humanly possible to do and that the truth would finally set me free.

While on the stand, I had my notes to refer to when asked questions requiring more details, such as times, dates, etc. It was like having a security blanket right by my side. I didn't want to forget a key point or confuse a date, causing what I said to be questioned and then invalidated. I firmly believe had I not kept such a detailed journal of events, along with photos, I would have stumbled under such pressure and possibly not been as powerful in my delivery of these horrible events that were so very much a part of my existence. When I glanced up to reply to his lawyer's question(s) and saw my soon-to-be ex, I no longer viewed him sympathetically as the man I married; rather, I saw him only as an enemy, my torturer and abuser.

There was no time during this court hearing for me to break down and cry or to show any signs of weakness and fear in front of this man. I remained steadfast and focused over and over again on the events that led me here. In the end, I was victorious, not only for myself but for my children as well. Our lives could now move forward in a positive direction

As I left the courtroom, people sitting there waiting for their case to be called were smiling, and some congratulated me, wishing my family and me the best of luck. I hugged my girls, and then the tears flowed down my cheeks. We were free, and all of this could be put into the category labeled the past. What an enormous burden to be lifted from my body and soul. There simply were no words then to describe that feeling, as there are none now. I walked out of that courtroom with my girls head held high and finally at peace.

The house that I worked so hard to maintain and keep was now mine. The children would not have to move or give up anything again. Our lives were ours; no one could or would ever destroy this again. I now can change the locks, finally helping to keep us safe again.

On the ride home, I could feel my legs still shaking, as were my hands. It had been quite an ordeal to live through. I drove home for some time in total quietness. I thanked God and my guardian angels for helping me through this. Ironically, the song "I Will Survive" came across the radio, which had been my theme song throughout this tumultuous ordeal. Barry Manilow's song "I Made It through the Rain" followed, and I was sure it was as if my heavenly angels were sending me a sign to say, "You did it, girl! You are a survivor! Now go and enjoy your life!"

There were other hearings that I had to attend to, but none were as stressful as what I had just been through. During this process for the criminal charges, my soon-to-be ex had a heart attack, and his lawyer contacted us at the courthouse while we were waiting to be heard. This caused for the case to be rescheduled, which meant another day of lost income to return to court.

During the time of his recovery, the two lawyers were battling things out, and because this was his first offense coupled with being in poor health, it was suggested that he be placed on five-year probation and that he not be permitted near me. If he saw me in a store, he was to leave, and he could not see the girls at the house. His pickup now was at the police station. His attorney also said that he was going to move closer to his brother's home, which was not in Pennsylvania. I think because they felt he wouldn't be living close to us now, the judicial system would try and give him another chance. Who really knows what the logic was, but I wasn't out for him to be in prison; I just wanted him to be far away from me. If moving to New York achieved that goal, then fine with me.

The custody hearing for the girls granted me primary custody with their father having partial custody rights, and we were ordered by the court to participate in the court conciliation and evaluation services, where there were scheduled meetings with each adult and then with the children. Because I was fearful that my ex would force me off the road—and with his past history, that would not be impossible—I was afraid to meet with him, but I would only if I could leave a half hour before he did after the meetings. That wasn't a problem for the courts; however, he refused to meet with me. When I had to take the girls to have their session with their father, I was permitted to leave the session one half hour ahead of him with the children to assure my safety. He would meet with the two girls on his own, and then I would meet with the girls on my own.

The courts validated my fears about him after meeting him for a few sessions and suggested he seek counseling, which, of course, he refused. The report stated that he's an angry man who finds fault in everyone else, and he will never be happy or at peace the way he is. Truer words were never said.

Chapter 20

AN UNEXPECTED CHRISTMAS SURPRISE

I refuse to be subjected to your mind
games and lies. I will not play a part
in your constant drama. You will not
manipulate me, nor will you control me.

—Unknown

During our many sessions, it was determined that my ex blames others for his behaviors and doesn't see himself at fault at all, which can be dangerous. He refused outside counselling, which would have helped him because, again, he feels the world is wrong and not him. After these sessions were complete, the recommendation was that the children *do not* have to go with their dad if at any time they feel uncomfortable. This made me feel safer for them as they could not be forced to go if they didn't want to.

This statement from the psychologist came in handy when I was ordered to appear in court by my ex for being in contempt of the custody agreement. The girls on this particular occasion did not want to go with their father and his live-in girlfriend. He took this to mean that I was interfering with his time with them, which was not the case. So during Christmas week, I was ordered to appear in court or be held in contempt. I couldn't believe that once again, not only our holiday was being ruined, but he wanted me now to be placed in jail.

Christmas has always been a special holiday for the children and me. It was a happy time of year, filled with excitement and anticipation. The lights, decorations, the magic of Santa Claus, waiting for Santa Claus to ride down our street on the fire engine stopping in front of the house for the kids to tell him what they wanted for Christmas, and then getting a candy cane from Jolly Old Saint Nick, picking out our tree and decorating it, baking cookies, visiting family and friends, exchanging Pollyanna gifts all made this holiday one of our favorites.

I did whatever I had to so that my children had that magical Christmas that I always had growing up. I pawned my jewelry (high school ring, gold bracelets, necklaces, engagement and wedding rings from my first marriage, earrings) that held sentimental meaning for me, and under normal circumstances would never have sold as they were my treasures, my sacred memories. I worked extra hours at my second or third job, memorized my kids Christmas wish list, put items on layaway, and was able to give them a fun-filled day. I was determined to give my children a beautiful Christmas filled with happy memories, and I knew that I'd have to do this all on my own. So to get notification that I had to go back to court the week of Christmas was alarming. I questioned myself, *Would he really want to put me in jail for contempt at Christmas?* Of course he would, and so I had to be on my guard yet again and ready once more for yet another battle.

I could not afford to employ a lawyer this time as I was so heavily in debt from all these hearings, so I gathered up the facts as well as my courage and decided I would take him on myself. Let me be clear: I did not stand in my daughters' way about going with their father, but I did respect their decisions, and that is what led me to this. I would do it again, if faced with this, because I would never force my children to do something they felt uncomfortable doing. They knew they were safe with me.

Since the girls were the focus of this hearing, I decided that they needed to accompany me in court. I didn't subject them to the courtroom scene during the hearing as this really wasn't the place for a nine-year-old and an eleven-year-old, but they were coming, and if the judge needed to speak to the girls and hear from their mouths why they didn't want to go, then they would be there. I asked my oldest daughter to come to sit with the girls in the lobby while I was in the courtroom, and it was nice having her moral support.

My hearing began, and I had to explain why I didn't send the girls. Of course, his lawyer was there, doing all the talking and questioning me as if I were the criminal. The banter went back and forth, and I tried to remain focused and calm, which was difficult. His lawyer tried to convince the judge that I was poisoning the girls against their father, which I vehemently denied.

It was at this point that I gathered up my courage and addressed the judge with this question, "Your honor, would you like to speak to the children?" His lawyer was taken aback and quickly interjected that he had no knowledge that the girls were here or wanted to speak. I told him, "Since you want to have me arrested over the Christmas holiday, leaving the girls without their mother for Christmas, and since they are the ones that didn't want to go, I feel they should be the ones to speak."

The judge wasn't too happy with me at first because I think she thought this would be a simple cut and dry case, but after I said that, I also said that we had been ordered to attend a court mediated counselling program, which we did. This document, which I had in my hands, clearly states by the court appointed psychologist on page 7 the following: "I would recommend that the children not have to go with their father if they do not want to."

I also said, "with all due respect, I followed the court orders and went through this counseling, and I would appreciate if the judge would take a few minutes and speak to the girls privately." I sensed that the judge wasn't at all pleased with my comments or my confidence, but my life and my children's lives were on the line, and I felt I had nothing to lose. It was my thought that if I am being sent to jail, I have one phone call to make, so I'd make it to the local newspaper/media to run a Christmas story about a single mother, who is a survivor, fighting for her children, and who now has been sentenced to jail over Christmas while her abuser was set free after trying to kill her on Mother's Day. That was the plan I would employ if I were sent to jail. Where is the justice here?

His lawyer was upset, and he did his best not to have the judge speak to the girls. Thankfully, the judge asked me to bring the girls in, and she would speak to them privately in her chamber before reaching her decision whether I was in contempt or not. His lawyer said that the girls' father should be permitted to be in the room, and the judge denied that request, so the lawyer said, "Then he would be there," and she again denied the request.

Both girls went into the judge's chamber, and she spoke to each of them. When she had the girls return to their older sister in the lobby, she made her decision, and when that gavel came down, my heart dropped. She stated that the girls were "afraid of their father and his anger, and they did not want to go with him and his girl-friend." They weren't comfortable about the way the adults behaved in front of them. She then ordered that they would never be forced to go unless they wanted to, and that I was not in contempt.

What a happy verdict that was for all of us. We left the court-room and had a nice lunch. I never questioned what they said to the judge because I respected their privacy. I simply asked how they felt, and they said they were glad that they couldn't be forced to go any-more. It was a Merry Christmas for our family!

I requested, when my divorce papers were finalized and signed, to take back my maiden name, in which my request was granted as I wanted nothing of him to negatively impact my life going forward. I signed the documents that granted me this wish, and that infamous pen that I used that day to free myself from his chains and his name is safely locked in my safe. With a stroke of the pen, I was a free woman.

It's a new day, one where my daughters and I live in a healthy environment, full of laughter, family, and friends. Those torturous days are behind us, and our future looks much brighter. I still have the scars from a turbulent marriage, built a wall around my heart so as not to be hurt again, and I'm always on guard; however, in time, I feel confident that this will lessen, and I will be able to trust again. This is my fervent prayer.

Chapter 21

ON THE ROAD TO A
NEW BEGINNING

I love the person I've become because
I fought to become her.
                                        —Kaci Diane

The time came when I could return to college and pursue my career. I would now be able to focus and concentrate on my studies without the fear of being hurt or embarrassed and without the fear of having my work or books destroyed. If I wanted to spend all day on a Saturday doing schoolwork, then I could. If I wanted to stay up late working on a paper, I could. There was no one who could hold me back anymore. I was on the road to being successful, and I couldn't be happier.

I started out by taking one college course while working, and then I ventured into taking two courses. It was tough, but my mind was set that I would graduate and have my BA in teaching along with my special education certification. As it was getting closer to seeing the end of the road, I sped up my graduation date by taking four courses.

Before I knew it, my graduation day was here, and I did it! My family came to celebrate this journey with me. Not only did my dad come to my graduation and my four girls, but my sister-in-law from my first marriage surprised me and helped make this accomplishment even more special. She is the sister of my first husband, and thankfully, we always stayed close. Even though my first marriage didn't work out, my mother-in-law (who since passed away) and my sister-in-law have always stayed in touch and close to me and my girls. We were and will always be family!

Walking in procession, looking up in the stands at my family cheering me on was a moment that I will cherish forever. When my name was called out to receive my diploma, I could hear my girls screaming my name. Tears welled up in my eyes and for the first time in quite a long time; I was proud of who I was. I now was dually certified (regular education and special education) to begin teaching. It was a moment that I honestly didn't think would come to fruition, and here I was, accepting my diploma and having my family present for this monumental moment.

My thirst for learning continued to grow, and I knew that I would stop at nothing. I immediately registered for my master's degree and took as many courses as I could each semester. I needed to care for my family and provide them with the security of knowing that no one or nothing would take their home from them, that now we would always have food in the refrigerator and cabinets, and things would work out. We no longer needed to depend on helpful hands to give us food, which we were thankful for, believe me, but now I could do it.

We had so many loving people who helped us through the dark days. One of our local stores provided us with pizza and sandwiches when I didn't have the means to pay. I would pay him the bill on my paydays. He never wanted to hear that my family was hungry and was always there for us. To this day, I am eternally grateful to him and have remained a loyal customer. The higher my education, the better I could provide for my children. These kids deserved this security, and by God, I was going to make it happen. I couldn't do this for my oldest two girls when their father and I divorced the first time, and I know they were hurting to give up their friends and lose their home, and I was determined that whatever I had to do, this would not happen a second time. I was the breadwinner, and I was not going to lose this house.

After I won the house, which I paid for, my father and brother began working to make improvements. I had new siding and new windows installed, giving the home a new look. I was wiping away any reminders where I would have flashbacks to what took place in this house. Our home was alive again, with friends and family stopping by and laughter, something that had been missing all these years. The girls had sleepovers, pool parties, and life was good finally!

Life continued with everyone busy either at school or at their jobs. Holidays were enjoyable the way they were meant to be. This was the life I wanted my girls to have! I didn't have the financial means to shower them with expensive vacations or gifts, but what I did have was a heart full of love, and I think they knew I would do anything to protect them. Maybe someday, I'll have the means to shower them with all the nice things in life that they lost out on in their youth.

Our lives were busy, each daughter pursuing their careers and beginning their own lives. Marriages, babies, career moves are a huge part of our lives now. Each one of us survived the tumultuous memories of years past, and our home is now a place of refuge, peace, and joy. It was as if the house felt the release too from all those stressors. If only these walls could talk, oh what stories they would tell.

I am now the proud grandmother of eleven beautiful grandchildren. The joys these children have brought into my life are immeasurable. I have had the honor to witness their births firsthand, coaching my daughters as they brought their sweet babies into the world. My prayer with each birth was that God always spare them the heartache of being seriously hurt in a relationship. I would take the pain repeatedly rather than ever have my loved ones go through this. I hope as they mature, that they make smart choices before entering into a relationship. I can guarantee you that I will always be there for them as they are my world. I love each one in a special way and appreciate their uniqueness. I have been richly blessed. I may be alone as far as a spouse goes, but I am surrounded by love from my children and their children, and for that, I am so grateful.

Life repeats itself. Now I attend dance recitals, sports events, concerts, graduations for my grandchildren as I did so long ago for my own four daughters. Life is beautiful, and to be blessed with being a part of your grandchildren's lives makes it even more so.

My daughters are always worried about me being alone and check in on me constantly. The roles seem to have reversed with them worrying about me. I am fine being alone. I am kept so busy with teaching and maintaining the house that my quiet times alone are cherished.

Would I like to have a special someone to go to dinner with or share his company, of course, but that is not in the cards. I am still in love with my first husband, and he is now married, so that dream is gone. I learned a valuable lesson from my dangerous, almost deadly, past relationship, and I will not settle for anything less or anyone else.

Chapter 22

LIFE IS FULL OF SURPRISES

*If you are lucky enough to get a second
chance at something, don't waste it!*

I had set my goals on obtaining my master's degree, and so I returned to the books and put all my empty nights into studying to achieve this goal. I had the support from my daughters as well as my dad. He was always telling me to continue with my education and to believe in myself. I knew this would be a tough ride, but it would all be worth it. I started taking two courses a semester while working full-time. It gets harder as you get older, but there was a force inside me that kept me driven to reach my goal. I wasn't going to let my past hold me down, and so I was on the path to prove that no matter what, I would and could maintain straight As and carry a 4.0 average. Tough goals, but they were my goals, and I was determined to do it.

One day while at school (teaching), I felt sick, and I knew something was wrong. I called the doctor, and he told me to head straight for the hospital. He was fearful that I was having a heart attack. I did as I was directed, and not thinking, I drove myself there, and when the emergency nurses took one look at me, they put me in a wheelchair and took me right back. I had been so accustomed to taking care of myself because I didn't have any other choice in my previous relationship. I drove myself to the hospital years before when I was hemorrhaging because if I didn't, I would have bled to death. And now I was fearful that I was having a heart attack as my chest pains were severe. I was in charge of my life once again.

Several tests were run, and I was admitted for observation and further testing. My children were called, and they were at my bedside. The look on their faces told me that I was in real trouble. They were scared, and so was I. I prayed that God please spare me, after all that we went through, to give us some happy times now to share.

Needless to say, I knew that I had my final paper to submit to college, and this counted as my final grade, and so I asked my daughter to bring me my books and laptop so I could finish in time. She was hesitant to do as I asked, and I begged my doctor to please let me fill my time with doing the paper that I needed to do. He finally conceded to allow me to do this, only if I stopped and took breaks to rest. At this point I would say whatever he wanted me to say just as long as I could get my paper done.

And so, my daughter brought all my classwork to me in my hospital room, notified my professor where I was and that I would have my final delivered to him by the deadline. I worked tirelessly on this assignment, completed it on time, and my daughter delivered it as promised. I got an A in that course, and life was good! The doctor couldn't believe how determined I was to do this assignment, but then, he didn't know about my past.

I was transported by ambulance to another hospital for additional tests and a heart cauterization and then transported back to the hospital where I was first admitted. Test after test were given, and I was beginning to feel like a pincushion. Thank God, all tests came back negative, which was such a relief. The result was that all this pain and numbness was due to stress, which caused muscle spasms of the heart. Wow, who would ever think that stress could do so much to your body? And who would think that I had stress in my life?

I was finally released, and my daughters wouldn't allow me to do a single thing when I got home. They cared for my every need even when I told them that I was okay. It was a scare, I will admit, and I knew that I wasn't ready to leave this world yet. I go for yearly checkups, and I am fine. I had to learn how to relieve my stress by taking a walk to clear my head, listen to music that was soothing, or just put everything aside for a while and sit back and chill, hard as that is.

Years of studying, papers to submit, exams to take, presenta-
tions to make, and the day came when I was graduating once again
with my master's degree and a 4.0 average. *I did it!* It was exciting to
see how happy and proud my dad was when I achieved my goal. I am
so thankful that he lived to see me accomplish what I did. I chose not
to attend my graduation and walk down the aisle because I felt like
I was a little too old to be mixed in with all the younger graduates,
and just knowing that I made it and had my diploma was enough
for me. Of course, I never told my daughters or my father that I was
supposed to walk in procession, or they would have forced me to go.
They learned this after!

Soon after, my father's health began to deteriorate, and my
brother and I were worried about his living at home alone. He really
didn't want to leave his home, which I understand, but he needed to
be around family now. It was at the point where he either moved in
with my brother or me, or he would have to be in a nursing home,
and I was not going to have that. I always promised both of my parents that as long as I am alive, they will not go to a nursing home.

After many discussions, he finally agreed to move in with me.
My home was better suited for his needs as he didn't need to climb
stairs. The bedroom, bathroom, kitchen, and family room were all
on one floor for him. Getting in and out of the front door was easier
as he didn't need to walk up or down steps. We kept his home so he
felt he still had his own home, and eventually, after his passing, we
sold the property.

My daughters were wonderful, helping with the care of my
dad. They made up schedules as to who would be with him on what
days, time schedules, and feeding schedules, and so forth until I came
home from work at four o'clock, and then I took over.

He loved looking out the front window and watching the kids
outside. He was content, and I believe he knew how deeply he was
loved. My dad was always worried about me, his little girl, and how I
would make it. He was my rock and the man I could always rely on,
and now he was coming to the end of his life, and we both knew it.
He would squeeze my hand and tell me how proud of me he was and
that he wished he were rich so that all my worries would be gone. I

told him repeatedly that I am rich in ways far more important than money. I have been loved my whole life by him, and money cannot buy this. His eyes teared up as did mine, and I understood what he was trying to say without really saying it. He worried about me, and he knew that he was always there whenever I needed him, and his concern was whom could I turn now if he wasn't there?

Strangely enough, my two older daughters told me that my first husband, their father, just lost his wife from cancer. I told the girls that I was sorry to hear this, and if there was anything that I could do to help him, I would but that I would not be going to the viewing/funeral but they of course should. I said that I would send him my condolences in a card, but they could relay it to him in person should they so choose.

After a few days, I sent him a card and told him if he ever needed a friend to share a cup of coffee with and talk, I was here for him. I included my cell phone number to call if he wanted. I honestly never expected to hear from him or receive his call, and then out of the clear blue, his voice was on the other end of the phone. It took me back for a minute as I hadn't heard his voice in so many years. Could this be possible that our roads would be crossing again? He said, "Is this Debbie?" to which I replied, "Yes, who's this?" He chuckled, and I knew instantly that it was him. I agreed to meet him that evening for dinner.

As I changed my clothes from work and prepared to meet him, I felt like a young girl again, nervous and yet excited. I had been single and on my own for fourteen years and now I was going out with a man, a very special man. Questions entered my mind like, "What would he think when he saw me?" "Would we be comfortable with each other again?" "Would the conversation flow easily, or would it be like meeting someone for the first time?" "Would my heart flutter like it did so long ago?" The only way I would have these questions answered was to meet him.

Driving down to meet him, these thoughts and questions filled my head. I was happy and yet scared about meeting him after all this time. I was free; he was free. I knew once I looked into his eyes that I could tell whether or not the love we once shared would still be there. His eyes told so much.

As I pulled into the parking lot and walked up to the restaurant, my heart pounded, and I prayed that I looked good when he saw me. I wasn't that young teenager any longer. I was much older now. I opened the door, and standing there in the lobby was the man I loved—then and now. He smiled and walked toward me. It was like we never were apart; we talked for hours, laughed, cried, and shared so many stories. He confessed that he was afraid to call after all these years, afraid of how I'd feel toward him.

He then told me that he confided in his sister, whom I remained very close to, and she advised him to call, reminding him, "What do you have to lose?" His sister knew that I always loved her brother, and the pain that I endured from his affair and then the divorce was still raw. I was so happy that she told him to call me.

Our meeting was everything that I hoped it would be and more. We lost track of the time and basically closed the restaurant. We were oblivious to the fact that no one else except the employees were left, that the staff had swept the carpet, placed the chairs up, dimmed the lights, and turned off the music. Once the music stopped, we realized it was time to leave, and so we stood outside in the parking lot, continuing our conversation until the restaurant's outside lights were dimmed.

As he walked me over to my car, he gently kissed me and asked if we could see each other again. Be still my heart! I must be dreaming! I found my love again, and I was being given another chance for happiness and love. He asked if he could call me again, and of course I said, "Yes, You better." I was on cloud nine, and I couldn't wait for our next meeting. When we kissed to say good night, the love that was felt in that kiss was so warm and passionate. Those soft kisses quickly lead into a passionate one. The kiss said it all: we never stopped loving each other. I found my true love once again, and I was not letting him go.

Our love was renewed, and it was a new beginning for the both of us. What a wonderful journey we were about to embark on together. The feelings that swelled inside me were unbelievable. I had to pinch myself over and over again on the ride home; it was a dream come true, and I was so thankful that I answered that phone call, the call that forever changed my life and his.

I believe in fate, that God has a plan for you and finds a way to help you see His plan and then follow it. He put us together when we were young, and we somehow lost sight of His divine plan. We lost sight and went our separate ways—blame it on our youth—but God never gave up on us. He knew we were meant to be together. He knew our love for one another never died, and so He tried again and succeeded. We are truly meant to be together because our love is one of a kind, and it continues to grow stronger each day.

He called the following day and every day thereafter. We both had our work schedules to keep us busy during the day, and just like young lovers, we thought about each other and longed to be together again. I felt like a teenager all over again, silly and so in love, counting the hours until we would be together.

My dad needed to be hospitalized for a brief period of time, and I visited him nightly. One evening while I was sitting with him, he noticed a police officer standing in his doorway. He said, "Debbie, is that a policeman at my door?"

I glanced up and saw that it was Terry. I smiled and told my dad, "Yes, Dad. It is Terry."

Dad looked both surprised and in shock as Terry approached his bedside. He said, "Hi, Chief. How are you doing?" Terry always called my dad Chief, and my dad sat up straight in his bed and gave Terry a warm handshake. It meant so much that Terry thought enough to visit my dad as my dad was always close to him. They talked about the good old days, and then my dad looked at me with a puzzled look as if to say, "How did Terry know I was in here?" I could tell by the look on his face that he was confused and that is when I told Dad that Terry and I were back together again. His eyes were teary, and he said he was so happy to hear that.

Terry stayed with us for a while longer and then had to return to work. Dad and I shared some father-daughter moments talking about how Terry and I got back together again and how strange life is. Dad said that he was thrilled with our reuniting and how he felt at peace because I had Terry back in my life. There was a look of peace that came over him as we spoke about life and how fate has its way of bringing people together. It was a good visit.

Then as I was about to leave for the night, my dad told me that I needed to listen carefully. He said that after he passes—and only after he passes—am I to go down to the rec room and over by the heater, push up the ceiling tiles, and remove an envelope, which was there. That was all he said. I told him I don't want to talk about his passing, and he very strongly told me to listen to what he was saying. I assured him that I was listening and that I would follow what he said, but my curiosity was now aroused. What was he talking about? What was so important that I had to promise him that I would do what he asked? Hopefully, I wouldn't find out for many more years.

The following day, I was able to bring my father home with my brother's help. Both my brother and I cared for Dad and were always there for him. We were blessed with a wonderful father, who was always there for us, and now we were returning the favor. My dad knew that he was deeply loved by his children and grandchildren.

My birthday came a month after we met again, and so when he arrived at the house with several presents for me, I was shocked. My father and daughters were here for my birthday, and when they saw Terry and me together, they knew I finally found my happiness. He showered me with so many expensive gifts that I didn't know how to react. He spoiled me with a new television for my room and a laptop. I can't remember the last time I was made to feel so special. How can I thank this man for showering me with his love and his gifts?

I smiled all night long, and then when they sang "Happy Birthday," they had no idea just how happy this birthday turned out for me. The gifts were wonderful, but the best part of this birthday was having him here to celebrate with me along with my girls. I can't remember when I felt this loved, this happy, and so special by a man. My children have given me so much love and support throughout the trials and tribulations over the years, and they have tried, in their own special ways, to always make me feel loved. Then to have the one man I loved with all my heart sitting next to me, holding my hand, kissing my cheek, wishing me a happy birthday alongside my children was the best birthday gift any girl could hope for. I was blessed!

One Saturday, we went out for a drive and stopped at Washington's Crossing. Terry pulled next to a tree and asked me if I remembered this spot? My God, what a memory he has and how sentimental he is. Yes, I remember this tree. It was where we picnicked with our families so long ago. These were happy times. Terry told me that every time he passed by this spot, he reflected back on our time together. He told me about other places that he reminisced about our times together, and I felt warm inside. It wasn't just me who thought about our happier times and remembered where and when we did certain things; he remembered too. We talked about our regrets, the poor decisions we made, and how we threw away our lives because we were young and foolish. What a waste of so many precious years, being with other people instead of each other. If I could turn back time, what things I would do differently as would he. But then, I would not have my two younger daughters, and that would have been a tragedy. Maybe we would not be as strong in our love and appreciate one another as much either had we not faced these obstacles.

Our conversation was deep, and our feelings of regret from those earlier years surfaced while standing under that tree, but soon reflecting back on how deeply in love we were back when we picnicked at this spot brought out all the love and happy emotions that never really died. This tree remembered all the love that we shared then and continue to share now. What a truly special tree. I could feel the presence of our deceased loved ones who once were with us that day, and I knew that they were smiling down on us and thankful that we were reunited. God took care of us and helped us find one another again, and I will be forever grateful for His blessings.

We love going to Peddler's Village, strolling from one store to another, and just taking a seat outdoors, watching people as they pass by. The Cock N Bull Restaurant held beautiful memories for the two of us. It was here that we celebrated family events with our parents, and so we decided to have dinner in the same room that we did so long ago. We ordered the same meal with the famous wedged salad and thought back to when life was good and so happy and when our parents were with us and how lost we are now without them. We share so many memories, both happy and sad, which makes it so easy to talk to each other. We are rarely lost for words.

Walking through the mall on Saturday, we passed by the jewelers, and Terry led me into the store. I knew it wasn't for wedding rings as we just got back together, so I was somewhat confused. He asked the sales woman to show him the beautiful emerald ring surrounded with diamonds in the showcase. It was similar to Princess Diana's blue ring with diamonds. He handed it to me to try on, which I did. He inquired if I liked the ring, which I did. I went to remove the ring from my finger, to which he replied, "It's for you."

I couldn't believe it, and before I could utter a word, he said, "It's for you, just because it's Saturday!" He kissed me, and I was speechless. This man never ceases to amaze me. I walked through the mall with him unable to speak. I couldn't believe that this just happened. Holding hands was something that I missed and envied as I would watch other couples as they walked hand in hand because this was what we used to do way back when, and now we are here holding hands once again.

This man was changing my life. He was always surprising me with something, and he never worried about the cost. He told me time and time again that I deserved whatever it was that he purchased for me, but I didn't want him to feel that he had to buy me things. I just wanted his love and companionship. Terry told me so many times that he had to make up for all those lost years and that he wanted to spoil me.

I loved the attention, but I never wanted him to feel that he had to spend money on me to make me happy. I am happy being in his company, taking walks or rides, holding hands, and sharing happy moments. All the money in the world or expensive gifts would never make me as happy as I am just holding his hand and knowing that he loves me. Money can't buy this. I have been without love for so long that I constantly feel like I am in a dream and don't want to wake up.

To hear my name lovingly being called, to feel his hand softly touch mine is a treasure. Years of being yelled and cursed at, hit and kicked are all that I have known for far too long; and now, being treated like a human being, a woman, is something I don't take for granted.

Chapter 23

REUNITED

Every love story is beautiful,
but ours is my favorite.
—Unknown

Funny how things your parents say over the years ring in your ears at certain times in your life. After my divorce from my first husband, my mother always would tell me, "If you love something, set it free, if it comes back, it was meant to be." These were wise words then, but they are so much more meaningful now.

Our meetings became more and more frequent. Being separated all those years from each other made us appreciate every day more, and we learned not to take anything for granted.

We were busy with our careers, him with the police department and me with teaching. We both had our own homes and the responsibilities that go along with it. He had to finish working on his house, completing the kitchen that he started remodeling, and packing up his deceased wife's items for her two daughters. I offered to help him gather up her belongings as I know he was dreading it. I suggested that before we boxed these things, he should have her girls go through the things in the closet and dresser to take whatever they wanted.

It was an odd feeling walking through the doors of his house. I felt uncomfortable at first, but I knew he needed my help to get things in order, and so I began by opening the curtains/shades to bring some light into the dark rooms. He had done so much work in this house. He laid hard wooden floors, was in the process of remodeling the kitchen and dining room. He was very talented.

He and I began cleaning up the house and worked on finishing the kitchen that he started. Once the house was in order, he called her daughters and asked them to stop over to take what they wanted. They agreed, and I stayed home that day. When they came into the house, they started asking Terry a lot of questions such as, was he seeing anyone? He felt that they could sense something was happening as he finished the kitchen and polished the furniture throughout the house. He denied that he was seeing anyone because he didn't want to upset them (more considerate than their mother was to me). They stayed for a short time and left. He told them that he would box up the rest of the things and drop them off, which he did. They were suspicious that someone else was in his life, but at the time, they had no idea it was me. Terry visited a few times with them at their homes, but there was a chill in the air when he chose not to stay overnight.

We continued to work on his house, painting the walls, buying new furniture and decorating for each of the holidays. The house came alive as did his craftsmanship.

As time went on, the girls (deceased wife's children) eventually found out that Terry and I were seeing one another. They had no idea that it was their mother who broke up our marriage, no idea of her evil plot; however, they soon found out when they contacted my daughters through social media. These two girls were calling me every foul name in the book, and it didn't take long for my daughters to set the record straight. My girls (one daughter from my marriage to Terry and one daughter from my second marriage) flatly said, "Don't you call our mother that name. It was your mother who broke up the marriage. She cheated and ran around with a married man, our father, so before you throw names out about our mother, you better be ready to hear the truth about your mother and the rotten things she did. Now our parents are able to be reunited!"

That was the end of the comments, and that was the last time my girls ever heard from them. I was proud that my girls stood up for me. Normally, I would have told them to consider the source and just let it go, but all those years built up inside me about what this woman did, and in a way, I felt vindicated that my daughters fought for me and told the facts to those that lived in a fake world. I also was relieved that I wouldn't have to see or entertain those two girls because they would be a constant reminder of what their mother took away from us and what my girls lost because it was all given to hers. So, yes, I am happy that they were told the truth and happy that another chapter of my past life could be closed.

It was now my time—time to be happy with the man I loved forever and he with me. We had been separated far too long, missed out on far too much, and having been given a second chance on life together, we were going to live life to the fullest and enjoy our moments together.

Chapter 24

THE LOSS OF A GREAT MAN

I truly never learned what the words I
miss you were until I reached for my
dad's hand and it wasn't there.

—Unknown

Dad was living with me for a brief period of time before we lost
him forever. He was cared for by his granddaughters in the day,
each taking shifts, and then I took care of him at night. My brother
was wonderful taking him for his checkups and doctor visits. The
family stopped in to visit and chat with him throughout the day. His
life was filled with family love and sharing memories.

Dad loved sitting by the front bay window, watching the birds
in the garden. He was a nature lover, and whatever this man touched
blossomed. He was failing, and I knew it, but it was a very difficult
thing to accept. He told me that he hoped he would see summer, to
sit out in the warm sun and watch the birds. It was now spring, and
I thought that his wish would come true; however, that was not the
case.

When I woke up for work this particular morning in April, I
went into his room to check on him and to see if there was anything
that he needed. He wasn't in his bed! I panicked and ran over to the
side of his bed that he slept on only to find him on the carpeted floor,
shaking. He had fallen out of the bed sometime in the early morning
hours, and he was unable to ring his bell or use his phone to notify
me that he needed help. I quickly went to him, held him, and spoke

to him to see if he could tell me what hurt or what happened. He just kept telling me how cold he was. I grabbed blankets, the quilt, anything that I could find and wrapped him as I proceeded to call Terry to come help me. Terry came as quickly as he could, and he just held my dad, trying to get him warm while we waited for the ambulance to arrive.

My worst fears were coming true. He looked bad, so weak and so old. I never felt as helpless as I did this morning. We followed the ambulance to the hospital; all the while, I knew this would be my dad's last trip. I felt sick in the stomach, and my heart was so heavy. How could I survive without this man in my life? I felt awful that I hadn't heard him when he first fell. How long was he on the floor? It haunts me to this day.

The doctors said that he wasn't able to come back home yet because he required round the clock care. I didn't want him to go to a nursing home. I promised him that he would not go. I asked about home care and was in the process of checking this out. My dad held my hand and asked me not to send him to a nursing home, and I again promised him I wouldn't. He just wanted to come back home.

I stayed with him most of the day, and when evening approached, he took my hand and squeezed it gently. I bent down and kissed him, and he whispered in my ear, telling me that he loved me, always has, and thanked me for loving him. He held my hand as tightly as he could and softly said to me, "You'll be okay. I am so happy that Terry is with you."

A strange feeling came over me as I realized that he was saying goodbye now that he knew his little girl would be safe, protected, and loved by Terry. My dad had always been my protector my entire life, and I strongly believe that he felt he could join my mother because I was in good hands with Terry. Tears flowed down my eyes and onto his face, and he cried as well.

He told me to listen to him and then directed me to where his important paperwork was and what I should do. He had everything written down in a copybook, guiding me step by step on how to handle his final affairs. The more that he spoke to me, the more I realized he was saying goodbye, and I cried even more. He also told me not to forget that there was an important envelope in his rec room, up where the ceiling tiles were, by the heater that I needed to take. He was making sure that he told me everything that he could remember and what he thought I needed to do. I just hugged and kissed him and held him until visiting hours were over.

When I kissed him good night, he repeated that he knew I would be taken care of now that I had Terry so that he was at peace. I kissed him repeatedly as I said good night, but I felt that this kiss was goodbye. I left and then walked back to his doorway and looked in. He had dozed off. I only wish that I had stayed that night with him—all night—so that he wasn't alone. This man, who was my dad, was so frail now, and I felt that he too knew that God was calling him home to be with my mother. I desperately wanted more time with him.

It was difficult falling to sleep when I returned home. All I could think of were the words that he spoke to me, and no matter how hard I tried to shake this awful feeling, I just couldn't. I loved this man more than life itself. He was my father, my hero, my savior, my confidant, my friend, my support system, and he was about to leave me. How was I ever to go on without him? I just didn't want to think about it; maybe if I didn't think about it, it wouldn't happen.

The following morning at 6:00 A.M., the phone rang, and I knew in my gut who it was and what it was about. I ran to answer the phone, and my worst fears were confirmed. The nurse sadly reported that my dad passed away quietly in his sleep. My God, this cannot be happening. I can't be without my dad; I just can't. I called my brother and Terry and relayed this horrible news as I headed out the door to see my dad.

When I arrived, the nurses hugged me and tried to prepare me for what I was about to witness. Entering that room knowing that my dad was gone was heart-wrenching. I hoped and prayed that they were wrong, but when I leaned down to kiss him, he was cold, and I knew he was gone. I just hugged him and cried like a baby. I hoped for one more day to tell him how much I loved him, to feel his kiss on my check, to hear his voice as he told me he loved me...just one more day, one more day, but then I know that one more day would never be enough, and I would want more.

I loved this man more than any words could ever express, and I found comfort in knowing that he knew it. We were blessed to have had such a wonderful father who loved and cared for his son and daughter as well as his grandkids, and he will forever be missed. My girls adored their Pop Pop (Pops) and took his death very hard then and even to this day. He had been their father figure after my divorces, and for them, it was like losing a dad. I can honestly say that there aren't many men in this world who were loved and cared about as much as my father, not only by his family but by everyone who knew him. He was a humble man with a huge heart. His words echo through our lives, especially when he would ask, "Have I told you lately that I love you?"

My brother and sister-in-law arrived and said their goodbyes too. We hugged each other and cried for what we just lost. Now we had the horrible task of making his final arrangements. Exhausted and saddened by our loss, the void in my life was ever so clear. I would never hear his voice again, feel his touch, enjoy his cooking, laugh at his jokes, and have a safe haven to go to for his wisdom and hugs.

Letting go of my father is still something that I can't do. He is everywhere I turn. This man was my rock. He knew when I needed a hug, a pat on the back, or a word of encouragement when I thought I couldn't go on. He instantly knew when I was short on cash and would stop by, open the refrigerator, leave, and come back with food for the girls and me. He made me promise him that we would never go hungry and that I would ask for help when and if I needed it. It was as if he had built-in radar when it came to me. His love was unconditional, and he never expected anything in return for his many acts of love and kindness.

Being able to pick up the phone to call him or stop by his house was now a thing of the past. God, I miss this man terribly, and the heartache still continues. I kept all the cards that he would send me, whether it was for a holiday, my birthday, or just a card that said, "I love you," and "I am so proud of you." To this day, I have one of his cards on my desk with words of encouragement and pride. This is whom I lost! My father and dear friend, and he can never be replaced.

Terry arranged to have a man who worked with him play the bagpipes as my father was carried from the church to his final resting place where he was reunited again with my mother, the one woman that he always loved. That is the only peace that I have right now, to know that my parents are together again.

At the cemetery, I was presented with the American flag that drapped his coffin by an Air Force Service man. I graciously accepted the flag and held it close to my heart, tears streaming down my cheeks because I knew how much my dad loved his country and this flag and all that it represented that I was just reverently handed. I knew how much my dad had sacrificed in World War II and just what an honor it was to have the flag presented to me, his firstborn child. I watched ceremonies on television where such an honor for a fallen serviceman was bestowed on a family member, but now, this wasn't TV or a movie; it was my life, and it was so real, and it hurt.

My dad had always told me that when he passes, if I don't do anything as far as placing flowers on his grave, which of course I do, that I had to promise him that his grave would never be without the American flag. That promise has been kept, and along with the change-of-season flowers (silk, of course, since my mother is also resting there), two American flags adorn the site.

I have come to realize over the years that death didn't take my dad away; he is still with me in everything that I do. In the beauty of nature, I see my dad; in the sunrise and sunset; as I walk along the beach, which we did so many times; in the songs that I hear; family gatherings; recipes that are now made by family that he was so famously known for; and in the sound of the birds or the beauty of the flowers as they pop up in the spring. My father is with me. He always said, "Remember me with love and happiness," and that is how I survive.

Now that my dad was laid to rest, my brother and I had the task of selling his home. I wish that I had the means to have purchased the home that we grew up in, but I didn't, and so it had to be put on the market. Fortunately, my brother was able to do the repairs and upgrades on the house so that it could be sold.

Each time that I entered the house brought pain as my dad was no longer there, and it was just a reminder of what we once had. Every room held a memory of a time that I would never see again. It was painful going through things that were my dad's and deciding what to do with them. As I was cleaning and packing items up, I remembered what my dad told me about taking down the ceiling tile by the bathroom in the rec room. I headed downstairs and reached up, popping the tile where he had told me to go. My hands trembled as I reached there and pulled down an envelope. It had Terry's handwriting on it, and it had been addressed to my dad when Terry was in the Navy. What was in this letter? Why had my dad kept it all these years, over forty-one years? What insight did my dad have about my relationship and love for Terry?

Carefully opening the envelope with the navy insignia on it, which was now yellowed from age, I began to read the words written to my dad so long ago. He asked my dad how he was able to live without the one person that he loved the most, referring to when my father was in India on a job assignment and away from my mother, and now Terry, who was away from me in a faraway land. He continued with questions, "Did you count the days and did they seem to never come? I need your advice because it is just eating me away inside and I can't stand being away from Debbie. I love her from the deepest corner of my heart."

He continued asking my father for advice as to how to make it through this separation (and I never got to know what the answer was since I didn't know about this letter until after his death). I read and reread his words, and paragraph after paragraph, I saw how deeply this man loved me. He wrote that I was "that half that made him whole and the one that made him strong." He said that it was me who "kept him going day to day and that he lived for sack time (bedtime) as it brought us one day closer to being together."

How strange is it that Terry and I found each other again, and my dad had the insight to share this letter with me now? This letter is a cherished treasure that I now possess for two reasons: one, that my dad thought enough to save it for me to read, and then that I was able to read just how much I meant to Terry. Love is a beautiful thing!

Chapter 25

THE ACCIDENT

Start by doing what's necessary; then
do what's possible; and suddenly
you are doing the impossible.
                    —Francis of Assisi

One evening in November, while at Terry's home, we were getting ready to grab a bite to eat, and as we left the house, I tripped on one step outside and fell. I thought I broke my leg as I couldn't get myself up, and the pain was excruciating. Terry looked at my leg and foot and said he immediately knew that I broke my hip. He called 911 as he tried comforting me as we waited for the ambulance to arrive. An ambulance flew down the street and passed us by.

Terry called 911 again, and they said the ambulance had been dispatched, to which he replied, "I know. They drove right past us." He informed the dispatcher that he would stand in the street to wave them down but that I was in a great deal of pain. He did just that, stood in the middle of the street, and waved them to stop.

When the ambulance attendants and driver saw the pain that I was in, they apologized to me for having to put me on the stretcher because they knew that it would be very painful as they quietly told Terry it looks like my hip was broken. The ride to the hospital seemed to take forever. I felt every bump and every turn. The sirens were blaring, and the lights inside were so bright. I tried my best to think of anything but this pain. My God, the pain was unbearable. When would it go?

Terry followed the ambulance, and I was so happy that he was with me throughout this ordeal. He called the girls, and they quickly came down to be with me. I could see it in his face that my injury was bad as his eyes looked so sad. When the girls came, I saw the same look. I knew I was in serious trouble and that it wasn't going to be a simple fix.

I was taken down for x-rays, and the tech was so sympathetic to my pain. She apologized for the way I had to be moved for the x-raying of my hip. The simplest movement of my leg was torture. The pain was indescribable. She informed me that my jeans needed to be cut off since my hip appeared to be broken. I gave my permission and afterward thought, *These were brand-new jeans!*

Then what she said really hit me! My hip was broken! I heard horror stories about people who broke their hips, the recovery time, and the pain. I knew this was serious and that I was in for a long recovery. All I wanted right then and there was for this dreadful pain to end. I never had a broken bone my entire life, and now it was my hip!

When I do something, I really do it in a big way. I have given birth to four children, and I have to say, this pain was far worse. I just wanted someone to give me something to take the pain away. After my x-rays were through, I was wheeled out and had to wait for the doctor. It seemed like an eternity until I finally was given something for the pain. I don't remember much after that. I had to rely on Terry and my girls as to what occurred after the x-rays. They let me know that I didn't go into surgery right away. I stayed on a stretcher in the hallway for many hours, and my family stayed right there with me.

After the surgery had taken place and I was somewhat awake, I was in shock as well as angry when I was told by my family that there was another person who had to be taken into surgery first before my emergency surgery because this patient was having a tummy tuck that was scheduled. I couldn't believe it. I was an emergency. I was told that I had shattered my femur and broken my hip, and I had to wait until a tummy tuck was finished. *Wow!* Thank God I wasn't conscious enough to hear that one.

Surgery was performed the following morning, and after being in the recovery room, I was taken upstairs to my room. My poor family stayed with me the whole time. What a long night that was for them. As for me, I was finally out of it, and I didn't know what was happening thanks to my morphine drip.

When I finally came to and the surgeon came in to speak to me, I realized that the wait was worth it because he was excellent. As I said before, this pain was worse than childbirth; at least with childbirth, the end result is having a beautiful baby, but this was dreadful.

The recovery was a long one; learning how to walk again and being able to move my hip/leg like normal took a great deal of perseverance and hard work. The team of nurses that cared for me both in the hospital and at my home helped me get through this horrible experience and made me realize how lucky I was to be walking on my own again. It was a *long* road to getting back to normal. I basically had to learn how to walk again. I went from the wheelchair to the walker then the cane. It was torture most days, but I was determined to walk and more importantly, to walk without a limp. I later found out that the reason my recovery took so much longer was mine was not elective surgery; it was a traumatic experience, and the damage was bad. I kept reminding myself that this wasn't going to get me down, not after all the things that I have been through. I was a fighter, and I would fight through this battle and win, just like all the other battles.

How I could trip over one step and cause the damage that I did still baffles me. I came to the conclusion, which you might think is crazy, but I do believe his deceased wife caused me to fall as I was leaving his house. I feel strongly that she wanted me out of the picture, and her spirit didn't want me with him. What she failed to realize is nothing could or would ever keep me from being with the man that I loved now and have always loved. After having these thoughts filling my head, I immediately burned sage to ward off the evil and negativity that surrounded me. My daughters and I laughed about this when I shared this thought with them, but at the same time, they agreed that burning the sage was necessary. It was just an odd feeling that I had, and it was as if my instincts were telling me that I was right.

My recovery was long. I recuperated at home in the beginning when I had to learn how to walk again and maneuver myself around the house, and then when I was better at the task, I went to Terry's house so it would be easier for him getting back and forth to work. We went back and forth between both homes.

I had been introduced to his German Shepherd, Max, over a period of time. Max was a loving dog to Terry, but to me, I was a stranger and needed to gradually be introduced to him. Time went on, and Max and I became friends. When Terry left for work, it was Max who stayed by my side and kept me company. As soon as he heard the truck pull up out back, Max would dart for the door and wait to greet his master. It was comforting having him around, and I became very fond of him.

Sitting around the house, watching TV day after day was just not my style. I needed to be busy. My mind wanted to go, but my body wasn't as willing. I am just not accustomed to sitting around, and I needed to find something to occupy this period of recovery. I decided to take online courses and work toward my plus sixty credits since I have my master's. I worked tirelessly on these courses while Terry took care of me. He wouldn't allow me to do anything but my schoolwork. He cooked, cleaned, and did the laundry while I stayed at his house, and when I was home, the girls did the same. I am richly blessed having such a loving family and support system. The quickest way to recovering is to know that you are loved and cared for. It makes all the difference in the world. With their help, I was able to complete all these courses (sixty additional credits) and maintain an A average all within the nine months of being home.

It had been a difficult year. I lost my father and then sustained a terrible injury. My spirits were at an all-time low, and then summer arrived. I needed and wanted to get out and feel the ocean beneath my feet, to try and walk the beach like I did so many times with my father. Being housebound was driving me crazy, and I needed to feel the warm sun on my body and feel alive again.

I mentioned this to Terry, and to my surprise, he planned a beautiful vacation for the two of us to Myrtle Beach, where we stayed at Litchfield Resort. It was gorgeous, and after all these long months of recovery, I felt alive once again. I had never been to Myrtle Beach before, but I knew he had vacationed there many times. I asked him that wherever we were to stay that he promised me he hadn't stayed there with her as I couldn't handle that, nor would I want to go there. I didn't have enough sage to burn to ward off the evil spirits anyhow! He promised me that he hadn't because he couldn't afford this place then, so this was a new experience for the both of us.

That made it even more special. I just wanted to be able to experience new things together. It would become our special place. What an enchanting time we had. I felt alive once more, and that is a wonderful feeling! The only reminder of my accident was when I put my bathing suit on, and the scars were so raw and evident of what I had recently gone through. I cried, looking at my leg, but then I gathered my bathing suit cover up skirt and proudly walked hand in hand with my love. That outward scar was just another reminder of what a fighter I am and how strong of a person I have become.

We vacationed there the following year, and the excitement was just as new. It was our special place! Going on a vacation renews your spirit, and having been there before, I now had my favorite spots to see or dine at. This man always knows when I need a lift, and he is always ready to do whatever it takes to make me happy. I am so blessed having him back in my life, and anywhere that we travel to is paradise as long as he is there beside me.

Chapter 26

ON THE ROAD TO A NORMAL LIFE ONCE AGAIN

Never let your fears decide your future.
—Unknown

Summer vacation was over, and the time had come for me to venture back to work after my surgery. I was filled with different emotions, excited to be returning to teaching yet fearful of how I would handle a full day on my feet. I had been so accustomed to taking frequent breaks and even naps when I felt tired, but now, I would have to go a full day without those luxuries. It was rough getting back into the swing of things, and my hip and leg hurt; often times, shooting pain would creep up on me and stop me in my tracks. I had burning sensations on that side and at times would feel that I didn't have control over my balance. I felt like a drunk, unable to walk straight.

I was advised by my surgeon to wear sneakers to reduce the pressure, and this was another blow, probably more to my ego than anything else, because I was so accustomed to wearing heels to work. Terry purchased several different styles for me to change off into, but I really wanted to wear shoes again. It simply wasn't to be at this stage of my recovery.

That first year back was difficult. I loved being back with the children as they are the reason I entered this profession, but it really took a toll on my body. I kept reminding myself that next year would be better; I'd be stronger, and by then, I would have learned how to overcome a lot of the discomforts that were part of my daily life right now. My surgeon reminded me that I suffered a terrible blow to my body, and it would take time. Patience, determination, and positive thinking would get me through this! Those words were easier said than done.

Terry was approaching the end of his career with the police department after forty years, which was quite an accomplishment. It seems ironic how fate has its way. I was with him when he began this career forty years ago, and now today, I am with him again as his career comes to a close. We went full circle together. I was so happy for him as well as myself that he had a successful career and that it was our time to enjoy his retirement. His career span took him from a patrol officer, to highway, to being a detective, and finally a sergeant. One promotion after another spanned this career, and now the time has arrived when he signed off for the final time on the radio, and he became a civilian.

His retirement dinner was as it should be with his two daughters sitting proudly next to him along with me and his sister. His family was there for him, beaming with such pride. He was honored for all his years of service as he should be. I thanked God that he made it through all those years safe and unharmed. Now, he can do as he pleases and enjoy the life that he worked so hard to make.

We reminisced that night of his accomplishments, where he worked, what dignitaries and celebrities he escorted over the years. He performed in the Thrill Shows, led many a funeral procession for the fallen heroes as a highway officer, supervised sports events, and the list just goes on and on. I told him the many times that I was at my mother's grave site and would watch the processions of fallen police officers being led by the highway patrol to their final resting place, and all that time, Terry was part of the ceremony, a row or two away from where my mother was. How many times we actually crossed each other's path and never knew it. Our paths were always passing, and now at long last, our paths connected, and we are together as it should be.

We both still had our own homes and running back and forth between the two were taking a toll on me since I was still working in the suburbs. His home held too many memories for me, and I really didn't want to live there. The home was lovely, but the neighborhood was going down, which he agreed. The single house in the suburbs had more ground and a backyard where we could enjoy company and cook out. It also was a great place for Max, our dog, to run around and play. This house symbolized all that I had to fight for to keep it after being a single mother for fourteen years to be free from all the pain that I endured all those years. I didn't want to give it up, and I knew if we both worked together, making changes in each room of the house, it could be ours, no longer holding any of those memories of the past. So we worked on his house to get it ready to be sold, which it sold in four days.

With that sale, we focused on our home in the suburbs, changing the decor in one room after another, completely remodeling our upstairs, where Terry now has a music room, and I have a beach room, plus a new bathroom, adding a beautiful new fence around the property, patio, his and her sheds, fireplace, and updating all the appliances as well as furniture.

The transformation was amazing! Nothing looks like it once did, and that's a good thing. This home is our home, and because Terry is so crafty and creative, making it even more special with his special touch. Our home is amazing, warm, and welcoming, and it is finally a safe haven. There was still a mortgage left on the house, and Terry surprised me by paying it off. It is finally debt free, and it belongs to us! After all these years! Now when I lay my head down on the pillow, I can sleep peacefully, knowing that no one can take it away from us.

Life was good! Our weekends were filled with rides to New Hope, Washington's Crossing, and Peddler's Village. We spent hours walking in and out of the local stores, holding hands, and feeling like young lovers again. Time stood still for us, and we were simply happy being in each other's company.

When we went to the restaurant for breakfast, the waitresses would say how happy he looks now and that we both belong together.

They told me that we were a true love story and that every time they saw us, they felt happy after hearing our story. So many people said our life was a fairy tale and asked when we were getting married again. Funny they should ask because our new date was set. We would become husband and wife once again in the fall.

Chapter 27

THE SECOND TIME AROUND

I guess I never let you go because in
the back of my mind, I still believe that
someday we'll get our second chance.
—Unknown

The excitement of being married again was all-consuming. After living on my own for so many years and my girls all grown with families and careers of their own, I was ready to commit one hundred percent to my husband. How did I become so lucky? There was just so much lost time to make up for and so many new memories yet to make. We both were ready to embark on this next chapter of our lives. It really wasn't our second marriage to each other but rather a continuation of the first. We are so much more mature now, and we realize how precious life is and how sacred our vows are. No one or nothing was ever going to keep us apart. I felt such a strong pull to our guardian angels at that moment when Terry asked me to be his wife again. I know they were working their magic from up above as they did when they set up our first blind date so many years ago.

We wanted our wedding to be elegant yet smaller this time with family and close friends to join in our happiness. Now older, wiser, we sat down and planned our wedding, simpler than the first but just as meaningful. This time, our daughters helped with the arrangements, invitations, the hall, flowers, centerpieces, music, menu, cake, and desserts. We set our date for October. The hall was decorated in autumn shades of orange, yellow, browns, and burgundy with each table adorned with handmade centerpieces. It was very festive.

I had asked the judge, whom I was friendly with for many years, to please perform the ceremony, which she did. Her presence made it more personable and so much more special. There was excitement in the air, laughter, and genuine happiness. It was difficult not looking around the room and thinking about those who were physically absent that day. How we longed to have our parents, grandparents present, but in our hearts, we knew they were with us and have been all along.

My dress was full length, silver in color with a matching jacket. It shimmered in the light and certainly wasn't as formfitting as my first wedding dress. What time does to one's figure! Terry wore a new blue suit this time around instead of a tux. He too looked different from our first wedding. I didn't think I'd have the jitters on our wedding day, but I did. I never liked being the center of attention, and today I was. I could see that Terry was feeling the same as I was—both nervous, similar to our younger days when I walked down the aisle with my love waiting for me at the altar.

My wedding ring was gorgeous. The diamonds sparkled throughout the ceremony as did my heart. Terry's diamond band was sparkling too as we said our vows. We listened intently to every word that the judge said and completely understood the promises we were about to make to each other. Reverently, we committed ourselves to each other. We understood the loss that we felt being apart, and we vowed that this would not happen again. We would love and cherish each other all the days of our lives. We were beaming with love for each other, and I felt that everyone present saw it too.

When the time came to dance as a married couple, and I was told that Terry selected this song as our new song, I cried. What a thoughtful man to have chosen the song "After All" by Peter Cetera and Barbara Streisand. Listening to the words and seeing how well they fit us and what we have been through was as though the words were written just for us. "Well here we are again. I guess it must be fate…" I broke down and cried in his arms when this verse played "Two angels who've been rescued from the fall. After all that we've been through, all comes down to me and you. I guess it's meant to be forever you and me—after all."

He couldn't have chosen a better song to celebrate our wedding! We had so much to be thankful for. As we held each other close, clinging to one another, Terry whispered how sorry he was for the poor choices he made and how grateful he was to be holding me again as his wife. I too was sorry for what had happened in the past and how young and foolish I was not to have worked things out, but we were now whole again, and nothing or anyone would ever come between us again. The song, his words, the tender moment in each other's arms made me feel loved again, and I knew how truly blessed we were. I believe that our parents were instrumental in making this moment happen with God right by their side.

Family and friends enjoyed our celebration of love, as did we. Our photo album is filled with happy memories and moments. Having our children, grandchildren, family, and friends there to celebrate with us made this reunion such a joyous occasion. Love was truly in the air!

Life quickly returned to normal, back to work as usual, and Terry counting the days until his retirement. Not leaving anything to chance, I became less reserved and more adventurous, or at least I was trying. Terry loved riding, so he surprised me with all the Harley-Davidson gear I would need to ride with him on those beautiful clear days. I stepped out of my comfort zone and hopped on the back of his motorcycle for wherever he was about to take me.

I was quite surprised to learn just how much fun riding was, feeling the cool breeze hit my face, and for a brief moment, feeling young again. I know my girls were shocked to watch me mount the bike and take off for this adventure. The look on their faces said it all—total shock and disbelief that this was their conservative mother on the back of a motorcycle! We rode to New Hope, stopped to shop, and then grabbed a bite to eat before heading home. I never felt this free before, and I looked forward to the next ride.

Sadly, my rides became less due to my hip surgery, but we still took our rides, just shorter ones now. Terry didn't encourage the afternoon rides as much either, and I knew the reasons deep down inside. He was worried about my hip and causing more problems, but I was fine as long as the rides were kept short. I was happy that I ventured out of my comfort zone and tried something new. I enjoyed those moments and the lesson that it taught me: to let go of my fears and go for it. I found out how much I enjoyed those rides and would never have had the experience had I not stepped out of my comfort zone. I am ready for whatever adventure awaits me now!

Chapter 28

FULFILLING DREAMS

Magic is believing in yourself, if you can
do that you can make anything happen.
            —Johann Wolfgang Von Goethe

Terry had always enjoyed bowling and even excelled in the sport, but he chose to walk away from it after his father passed away. Although his love for the sport was strong, the memoires it held with his dad were stronger. When he entered the bowling alley, flashbacks of the special father-son times spent with his dad, practicing, playing in the tournaments were all too painful to relive. Instead of using these memories to continue on with the sport, he chose to put it behind him. He simply couldn't get past his loss.

Out of the blue, after we got back together, he announced that he wanted to get back into bowling. *Wow!* After over twenty-five years, he was ready to be a bowler again. I was thrilled and supported him one hundred percent.

Now the real challenges began as things drastically changed over the course of so many years. Lane conditions were different, equipment was not as he had remembered, and these were obstacles that he now had to face if he wanted to get back into the sport. He purchased what was essential to embark on this journey, coupled with taking a few lessons and practiced as often as he could.

Soon, he joined a league, and the rest is history. He has come full circle on two leagues—bowling in tournaments and loving the sport that he left so long ago. Of course, he has acquired many new bowling balls, which requires him to carry two bags all because lane conditions now monitor what type of ball is needed (as per him). Birthdays, holidays—it is always a new bowling bowl on his wish list. Happily, he has found an old friend again!

Our daughter surprised him for Christmas with a replica of the original bowling ball that he had used when he was younger and bowled with his father. She included a photo of that moment with her gift. To say he was shocked is putting it mildly—he was very emotional and treasures those moments. Once again, his father is right there beside him, guiding him, if in spirit only.

I too fulfilled a dream of mine: to own a new car, one that I could buy with my own credit, especially after the rocky roads I had to climb over the years. We went out looking for a new car for me, and as we were walking through the showroom, my eyes became fixed on one in particular. It was regal looking—shiny black, sleek lines, interior lights like a limo with the door handles that also light up, coupled with gadgets that one could ever hope for or even need. I didn't even know what make the car was, nor did I care. All I knew was this was me, and I wanted it.

Several people were walking around admiring its beauty, and I laughed and told Terry, "This is my car!"

He chuckled because he knew full well that I had no idea what type of car it was, as he asked me, "Do you know what this car is?"

I immediately replied, "No, but I know I want it."

He said, "It's a Cadillac."

Wow! Well I was set on buying my first new car, and if it was a Cadillac, so be it.

All my life I had secondhand cars, hand-me-downs, because I could never afford a new one. My dad gave me his cars whenever he decided it was time to purchase a newer one, as did my oldest daughter, knowing that I could never afford a car payment and maintain a house plus all the expenses that went with owning a home, and continue to support the family. I had been the breadwinner for so long, and my worry was just keeping a roof over our heads and food in our bellies. But now, the time had come, and I was able to think about what I wanted.

It was a beautiful and yet surreal moment in my life. I think the symbolism of finally arriving and being able to treat myself was overwhelming. Terry told me to call the salesman over and discuss price and terms to make this purchase. I was worried that maybe I would be denied due to my credit, and this dream would crumble right before my eyes, but then I talked to myself and said, *Take the leap and go for it*, and so I did.

The salesman said he would run my credit first, and then we could talk. The wait seemed to take forever, and then when he returned, he told me, "You can buy a Jaguar if you want! Your credit is top—excellent! Are you sure you want this car when you can have a Jag?"

Oh my God, was he really speaking to me! I jumped up and down in disbelief, eyes filled up with tears as I hugged and hugged Terry. I really made it; I finally arrived! All those years of sacrificing and struggling were now a thing of the past, a bad memory! To be able to come to this moment in my life was so uplifting. Life was turning around for the best! My hands trembled as I signed the papers. What a moment, a moment that will stay with me forever. Then Terry surprised me after I was approved on my own credit and put down a sizeable deposit to lower my monthly payments. I will never forget this moment!

My car left the showroom, and the keys were turned over to *me*! When we drove up to our daughters' homes to show them my new car, each one cried with sheer joy for me and how far I had come. Who would think that the purchase of a car would mean so much, but it did, not only for me but for my children as well. They knew of the many struggles, and this car symbolized that I made it! I never stopped believing that I would rise above all the pain and heartache. This was a visual statement of how hard work, positive thinking, believing in yourself, and sheer determination actually pays off. I hope my girls learned that lesson too as they saw their mother that day. Never give up on your dreams!

We continued to seek adventure and make our memories along the way when we purchased our RV when we went to an RV show. This vehicle has opened new possibilities for our entire family, creating cherished memories along the way. We've been to Myrtle Beach and Nashville, Tennessee, and this is just the beginning. There is so much of the USA to explore, and I am ready to embark on the journey. I have learned to leave my fears and worries behind me and started looking forward to new places to explore, new friends to meet, and more happy memories to fill our scrapbooks with. Life is an adventure, and I am ready to meet it.

Chapter 29

HEALTH SCARE

She stood in the storm and when the wind
did not blow her way, she adjusted her sails.
—Unknown

Our summer traveling plans were put on hold due to a health scare. I went for my yearly mammogram, followed by a biopsy and received the news that I always feared: I had breast cancer. Hearing these words from my doctor, my body went limp, lifeless, and at first, I was too much in shock to even cry. My husband sat beside me as we were given the devastating news, and once our eyes met, the tears flowed. How could this be happening? We just found each other again after all these years, and now cancer came to end it all. Oh my God, I couldn't believe the words that the doctor just uttered.

Thank God Terry was listening to her because all I heard was cancer. I missed everything else she was saying; *cancer, cancer, cancer* was echoing in my head, and nothing else was heard. The doctor said that my cancer was caught very early in the beginning stages, and the tumor was very small with an excellent prognosis. I was then given my options to consider for treating this horrible disease. I could have a mastectomy or a lumpectomy. That was a lot to think about and a huge difference in whatever my choice was. I wasn't about to have a mastectomy if the tumor was as small as the doctor said it was, so I chose the lumpectomy. The doctor told us to go home and think about which way we wanted to go. We left the office, and once outside, standing underneath the tree near our truck, I collapsed into Terry's arms and cried. The tears just poured out of me, and he assured me that I would be fine. I know he was as scared as I was and that he was putting on a front for my benefit.

On the ride home, I was very quiet. My mind was running away with all types of scenarios: What would this road now be like? Would I need chemo? Would I lose my breast? Would I die? Terrible thoughts ran through my head as I remembered the suffering my mother and Nanny endured from this dreadful disease. How was I going to be strong for my family? How am I going to tell my children and grandchildren so they wouldn't worry? Terry reassured me that it was all going to be okay, and just like the many other struggles that we endured together, we would pull through this one as well.

Doctors' appointments, radiologist appointments, and decisions to be made occupied much of the weeks ahead. I was determined that I would be informed, knowing step by step what was about to take place in my body. I needed to know my options, outcomes, chances for reoccurrences. I refused to be lied to, to have things sugarcoated. I wanted the truth, and I did my research, so I was well prepared when I met the medical team.

After speaking to the radiation oncologist, I left his office feeling much more confident that the outcome would be positive. He agreed that my tumor was very small, so a mastectomy was not needed nor was chemotherapy. Hope now began to fill my inner being, and I fought hard to remain positive. This doctor was just what I needed in my corner. He was thorough, honest, and did not rush me to see his next patient. I was important to him, and he spent as much time as I needed, answering my many questions and explaining the procedure. He gave me his number to call should any questions come up that I might not have asked him in the office or if I had any fears/concerns that he could help me through. I knew at that moment that I was in the best of hands.

My appointment with my surgeon prior to my surgery was filled with just as many questions as I had for my radiologist. She went over the procedure with my husband and me again and told us that more would be known after surgery, and if at that time my breast would need to be removed due to the spread of cancer, it would be done then. I was given a paper to sign, agreeing if that was the only way to rid my body of cancer, then that is what would be done. I realize that my breast is just a part of my body, and saving my life was most important, but it was also a part of being a woman for me. I kept having flashbacks of my mother and how she suffered after losing her breast, how the depression set in, and what a toll it had taken on her even though my father told her repeatedly how beautiful she was. I know what she felt as a woman and a wife, and it was so painful to watch. I left her office praying that this would not be the case for me and that the surgeon would be able to get all the cancer without removing my breast.

Surgery was scheduled, and I made my plans with school to be away from my class for approximately six weeks. My work family was so supportive and so loving. I am richly blessed because these people were right there through the good times and the scary times. It was a horrific ordeal, and they never forgot me. They always had words of encouragement, sent me flowers, cards, phone calls, prepared food for me, sent me books to read, and kept my mind occupied. They made contributions in my name in the hopes of finding a cure for cancer, and then they had special shirts made up with a pink Wonder Woman symbol on the front of the shirt and Team O'Neil on the back. They wore these shirts every Monday, remembering me. What a team! Tears of joy and disbelief consumed me as I saw the support these people had for me during this battle. I will be forever grateful.

One of the items that I cherished more than they could ever realize was a mason jar they made filled with individual quotes and good wishes to cheer me up on days when I needed it the most. The note on the jar read,

> Here's a little gift from all of us to you.
> Take out a message when you are feeling blue.
> In the morning or at night, any time you're not
> feeling quiet right. I hope that our words will
> give you some strength, for you Debbie, we'd go
> any length. The road will be rough, but not very

long. You'll come out a winner because you're so strong! NO ONE FIGHTS ALONE!

Some days, I would pull one saying from the jar, read it, cry, and then carry on with my treatment for that day. Other days, I found I needed to read three, four quotes or notes to get me through, sayings like, "Always remember you are braver than you think, stronger than you seem and loved more than you know." "You are the strongest person I know. If anyone can win this fight, it's you! I love you and I am here for you!" "Don't be strong, fight to win!!!" "For every mountain, there is a miracle!"

The special jar was filled to the brim with words of comfort such as these, and then another saying entered my mind one day as I was laying on the radiation table, looking upwards at the ceiling, and that was a saying that my mother kept on her nightstand from the time she was told she had cancer. I now live that saying, which is, "Let Go—Let God." I placed my fears in God's hand and prayed that this battle would be just another one that I came out the winner.

As the day of surgery approached, I was consumed with fear and a sense of uncertainty for my future, for what lied ahead. I had been used to being in charge of my life, and now I had to put my life in the hands of my surgeon and, of course, God. I came to realize that all the worrying in the world was not going to change what would be. With that in mind, I decided to take charge of my life as best as I could and put a smile on my face (and this was hard many days) and try to be as positive as I could. Was it easy? Absolutely not! Was it necessary? Absolutely yes, if I was to get through this. My loving support system was there, cheering me on.

When I came out of surgery, my loving family was right by my side. Knowing that I was worried about losing my breast to cancer, they happily told me that I did not lose my breast and that my cancer was now gone. *No more cancer!* The doctor assured me that she got all the cancer out and that she had to remove three lymph nodes to be sure that nothing was left in my body. I would have to undergo radiation, but chemo was not in the plans. Thank God! Again, those tears flowed from my eyes, but they were tears of relief this time. I still wasn't out of the woods, but the worst was behind me. I had to wait for the pathology report from my removed lymph nodes, and they came back with no signs of cancer!

After a week home recovering from surgery, I was ready for the next fight, which was radiation. I was a candidate for something called the balloon. The doctor inserted a device into my right breast where my surgery was, and that would remain in place until my radiation was finished. I had two rounds of radiation directly into my right breast through this device twice a day. I went Monday through Friday, once in the morning and once in the afternoon for five days. It was a tiring experience, but it only lasted five days instead of several long months.

I recall being told that humor was important in recovery. When I could laugh, I would look at myself with all the crazy wires protruding from the side of my breast, wrapped in gauze, and tucked into my very unflattering sports bra and think to myself how sexy this was. I had been accustomed to my sexy and stylish Victoria Secret bras with all the lace and flattering colors/prints, and now I was sporting this crazy concoction. This was a test in humility for sure.

Humor is the best medicine, they say; well, looking at me in my hospital gown was another test in humility. My first time going to radiation was an experience. I wandered into the men's waiting room instead of the women's and was quickly escorted to the correct changing/waiting area by the nurse. What a sight I must have been for those poor men sitting there in their own sexy attire. We laughed about this every time I headed to the changing area, and the nurses were sure to direct me to the correct area.

With all the emotional support that was there for me, I still had to enter the room where my radiation took place alone. As I changed into my gown in preparation for radiation and looked around the room, I was alone. I knew I was loved, and there were so many cheering for me, yet in the end, I had to prepare myself for the unknown. Looking around the room, seeing the machine getting hooked up to me, watching the flashing lights indicating that no one should enter the room as it was radioactive was frightening. As I looked up to the ceiling where there was a beautiful scene of trees and clouds painted on the ceiling tiles, I fought back many a tear. I kept telling myself how lucky I was and that this would soon be over. I believe in the power of positive thinking, and that is what I did day in and day out. I felt embarrassed and even annoyed at myself when I was feeling low because I was one of the lucky ones. My emotions ran all over the place.

When my radiation was completed, and I was declared cancer free, I rang the gong, signifying I was now a cancer survivor! The hospital staff was amazing and so caring. I truly was blessed with a very supportive team from my family, to my work family, to my doctors and my nurses. I made it because of the love that was showered on me, and I will be eternally grateful. No one should ever have to go through this alone. It rips at your heart and soul and plays havoc on your mind. I pray that soon, there will be a cure for this dreadful and hated disease.

I had a meeting with another doctor who would be the one to prescribe medicine that I would take for the rest of my life should I need it. Again, I was on a mission, and I researched the medicines that were commonly used in treating cancer. Some of the side effects were horrific, and I wasn't about to put myself through that, so I went to my appointment with a list of pros and cons to the various medicines and knew what ones I wasn't taking.

The doctor spoke about my cancer and how it was now removed; that my lymph nodes were all clear; and that from all my test results, he saw zero signs of any cancer cells in my breast. He went through all of the follow-up treatment plans, and as he mentioned one plan, he would comment, "This isn't for you."

He began speaking about medication, and that is when I told him that I definitely would not take a particular medicine because all the research on it was very harmful to other organs. He listened, commented that I apparently did my research, and seeing that I was adamant and even upset over taking this medication, he came back with, "Your cancer is gone. You are not a candidate for any medicine!" Wow! This is unbelievable and wonderful! What a relief. I was getting back to normal, and I was so grateful. I knew that nothing would be taken for granted again—nothing—and that I would live my life to the fullest because I was given the gift of life once again.

I always was a person who was prepared and did my research, and this was just another example of the importance of taking charge. You need to know your options and do your homework. I think sometimes doctors aren't pleased that we have so much information at our fingertips with the Internet, but I think it is critical to being well versed in the science of medicine. Being prepared, having the questions ready to ask during a doctor's visit, and knowing your options is something everyone should practice. It is our life, and there is too much at stake. I am glad that I was prepared and in charge of my life.

My husband stood with me and by me throughout this horrific ordeal, as did my children. I know that no matter how strong I was as a person, I couldn't have done this without them. They picked me up when I was at my lowest point, and they never let me feel sorry for myself. They were a positive force during this, and I love them dearly for their support. "With family and friends, with hope and faith, I AM A SURVIVOR."

When Christmastime rolled around, the girls (daughters and granddaughters) gave me a beautiful Pandora charm for being a survivor and then presented me with four pink balloons. On one balloon they wrote the message, "Life is what you celebrate—all of it." I was instructed to write something on the other three balloons. Each balloon, I wrote a message pertaining to being a cancer survivor, and so I wrote, (1) "Thank you for making me a survivor," (2) "Thank you for always being there for me through happy and sad times," and (3) was my message to my mother, who lives in heaven now with the angels, "To be as good a Mother and Grammy as she was."

We went outside, and as I looked up in the sky, I released the balloons and watched them soar to the heavens until I could no longer see them. It was a very memorable and touching gesture. I know I have said this many times, but I am so blessed to be so loved.

Chapter 30

ONE BATTLE ENDS AND ANOTHER ONE BEGINS

When you come out of the storm, you
won't be the same person that walked in.
That's what the storm is all about.
—Haruki Murakami

As we overcame my battle with cancer and celebrated the happy news that I was now cancer free, cancer decided that it wasn't finished with us yet. It veered its ugly head once more and attacked my husband. Shortly, in a matter of two weeks after my diagnosis of cancer, my husband was informed after blood tests that his PSA levels were through the roof and that prostate cancer was now something he needed to address. This wasn't going to be as simple as having a biopsy and then moving forward since he had two heart stints over the summer and was on medication that could cause heavy bleeding should he undergo surgery. His treatment plan was altered, and so he was put on hormone medication for six months along with a shot of Lupron every three months for two years.

A biopsy was a must in order to combat his cancer, so the risk was taken with a very qualified team along with his heart doctor to monitor, to locate the areas in need of radiation. Terry pulled through this like a champ, but I could tell how worried he was. I was as worried, if not more, than he was as I sat nervously with our daughter, waiting and watching for the doctor to let me know that he was okay. I was scared that I could lose the one man that I loved, and I kept reminding myself that I had to remain positive. I had to send positive thoughts out in the universe if I ever hoped they will materialize. I prayed and begged God yet again to help us through this ordeal and bring us some comfort as well as grant us many more years of being together.

Fear, anxiety, even sadness became the emotions that flooded through his mind as he waited for the biopsy results and what exactly his treatment plan would be. During this waiting period, Terry had to undergo emergency surgery. He had suffered through various degrees of stomach pain and went to the hospital. His appendix was about to burst and was caught just in time. He was lucky, but this caused his prostate cancer treatment to be delayed. Now, his fear was, "Would the cancer continue to grow? Would this delay create additional problems? Would it be too late to save him?"

He truly felt that his life was over. I prayed that this wouldn't be the case, and in my heart, I knew it wasn't. I understood his fear because I too lived it myself. Once he received the all clear to go ahead with the radiation treatment, he felt more positive that things were now moving in the right direction.

Unlike my cancer, which was removed, his wasn't. His would be eliminated through many channels, such as medicine and radiation. Radiation was a part of his daily regimen for two months, five days a week. He grew tired and worn out as the radiation continued. Our daughters took him when I was unable to as I had returned to work and had no time left to use since I had used so much up with my own cancer treatments.

He was never alone during the treatments, which made the journey less stressful. Terry said he "never thought it would end," as each day he got dressed and headed for the hospital. But like everything, there is an end, and luckily, his treatment was successful. For the next two years, he will be seeing the doctor for his quarterly Lupron injections and be required to have periodic blood work to be sure his levels are in the right range.

As I mentioned before, humor is key to a healthy frame of mind, and so on Terry's final day of radiation, when he too would ring the gong, signifying that he was now cancer free, I had T-shirts made up for us to wear in celebration. They had the cancer symbol with the words "RADIANT B & B COUPLE." Radiant because we both underwent radiation, and the "B & B" stood for "boobs and balls." The nurses laughed and said they would never forget us! Likewise, we will never forget them for their kindness, warmth, and love.

Like me, our daughter arrived that evening when the treatment was finished with four blue balloons for Terry to write a message and send to the heavens. He wrote: (1) "Total Cure Once and For All," (2) "First Day of the Rest of My Happy Life," (3) "A Long and Happy Rest of My Life with My Debbie," and (4) "Happy Ever After with the Love of My Life, My Debbie."

As he released the balloons and we stood outside, watching them glide up to heaven, we felt a sense of relief and noticed each other's tears as they flowed down each one's faces. God has been good to us, and we are so grateful.

Chapter 31

ADVENTURE AWAITS

Life can change so fast, so unexpectedly.
Love when you can, while you can,
and as much as you can.

—Love Matters

Summertime came, and there was nothing that was going to hold us back now from celebrating life. This past years' experience has taught me to put nothing on hold for another day, to live every moment, as nothing is guaranteed in life. We both were given a clean bill of health, and that was a gift! We prepared our RV for a vacation to Myrtle Beach filled with fun, laughter, and family. To be back on the white sands at the beach, soaking up the sun, walking the beach, and listening to the ocean was all we needed, simply enjoying the simple things in life that are so often taken for granted.

During our vacation, I decided to do things that I might not have done a year or two ago. I now was ready to take chances and be a little less fearful and a little more daring. After my hip surgery years ago, I had always been afraid to go into the ocean and get knocked down by the powerful waves. I worried that I wouldn't be able to get back up or that I would look foolish as I struggled to get back on my feet. Today, I didn't care. I rode those magnificent waves, got knocked down, and got right back up. It was as if I was reliving my youth, and I loved every minute of it. The grandkids were right there to help pick me up should I need help, and they laughed as one wave after another took me down. It was wonderful! I was alive again!

Another moment that will remain in my heart as a fond memory was holding baby tigers and feeding one a bottle, along with holding a baby monkey. My granddaughters sat with me and shared in this moment. We talked about this many times, and we all came to the conclusion that this was one of the best moments.

I rode in a helicopter during vacation around Myrtle Beach, which was a first. It was amazing. I ventured out each day, looking for something to try or do that I hadn't tried before, something like having a bucket list of things to try. We got our lives back again. We know how precious that is because we came close to losing it.

We will continue to celebrate our freedom from cancer and enjoy moments together. The chapter on my struggles and abuse are now in the past, as are the battles with cancer. This part of the journey is now over. Yes, there were speed bumps along the way, but they made me stronger. There is no finish line, and so I intend to love the journey! I am now looking forward to many more happy days with my husband, family, and friends. Life is what you make it, and I intend to make mine memorable!

Everyone has a story; don't be afraid to tell it!

About the Author

It was the author's belief in her heart that she was determined to rise above all the hardships and still remain positive and hopeful. She pursued her degree in teaching to just shy of a doctorate while her life was in turmoil. When others would have given up because that was the easy way out, she stormed ahead to fight these injustices. She endured many sleepless nights, cried many a tear, and fought many battles both in and out of the courts, while keeping a smile on her face and hope in her heart.

The lesson to be learned from her is to *never* let anyone tear you down and that all things are possible with hard work and determination. No matter what situation you are facing, you are the catalyst for the change in your life!

CPSIA information can be obtained
at www.ICGtesting.com
Printed in the USA
LVHW031447261120
672639LV00003B/237